HEARTS OF OAK, NERVES OF STEEL

Hearts of Oak, Nerves of Steel

Shipwrecks and heroism in the Celtic Sea

by

Ian Skidmore

First edition: 2000
Revised edition: 2007

© Text: Ian Skidmore

ISBN: 1-84524-094-4
978-1-84524-094-3

Cover design: Sian Parri

First published in 2000 by Gwasg Carreg Gwalch
12 Iard yr Orsaf, Llanrwst, Wales LL26 0EH
℡ 01492 642031   🖷 01492 641502
📧 books@carreg-gwalch.co.uk   Web site: www.carreg-gwalch.co.uk

Revised edition published in 2007 by Llygad Gwalch,
Ysgubor Plas, Llwyndyrys, Pwllheli, Gwynedd LL53 6NG
℡ 01758 750432   🖷 01758 750438
📧 gai@llygadgwalch.com   Web site: www.carreg-gwalch.co.uk

Dedication: To the Head Ferret – Abide with me, always.

Contents

Acknowledgements 7

Chapter One: 'The Doors of Death' 9

Chapter Two: The Most Fortunate Fleet 27

Chapter Three: Lifeboat Rescues 40

Chapter Four: Rescue 62

Chapter Five: Three Men in a Boat 81

Chapter Six: 'Devil Boats' 94

Chapter Seven: Search for Treasure 119

Chapter Eight: Fire! 124

Chapter Nine: The Welsh Captain Hornblower 133

Chapter Ten: Flotsam and Jetsam 148

Acknowledgements

Dr Cecil Jones, marine archaeologist. Wendy Cuerden for diligent research cheerfully made with splendid results. As with all my books, I am delighted to put on record my thanks to and admiration for the staffs of Llangefni Public Library (especially Helen Hughes), the Archives Departments of Ynys Môn and Gwynedd and the Daily Post library staff. The finest research team an author could hope for. Also for the painstaking and inspired editing of John Puw.

Chapter One

'The Doors of Death . . . '

'X...X...X...'

In the pitching wireless cabin of the *SS Princess Victoria* her radio officer David Broadfoot tapped out the international urgency signal on his morse key.

09.46 a.m. 'X...X...X *Princess Victoria* to GPK. Hove to off mouth of Loch Ryan. Vessel not under command. Urgent assistance of tug required.'

At GPK, the code sign for Portpatrick Radio Station, the signal richochetted round the room like little bullets of sound that had the base operators rushing for their own morse keys, summoning aid.

The *Princess Victoria*, a 2,694-ton car ferry, known in the British Transport Commission fleet as the 'happy ship', had left Stranraer with a crew of fifty-four and one hundred and twenty-three passengers, on the 35-mile passage to Larne at 08.06 a.m. on 31 January, 1953. The journey should have taken her a little over two and a half hours. Fifteen minutes out of port, she was fighting for her life.

Nosing out of Loch Ryan, five miles west-north-west from Corsewall, she had been hit by a northerly gale which gusted to seventy knots, whipping across the tide, creaming it into mountains of spray and raising mighty walls of green water.

10.30 a.m. 'S...O...S...GMZN'

GMZN was the call sign of the *Princess Victoria*. Broadfoot, the sender, was a 51-year-old who had served in the cross channel fleet between Ireland and Scotland since 1951. He was to spend the rest of his life in the cabin. All three hours of it.

On the bridge with his chief officer, S. Duckley, his second officer, L.A. White, and Leckie his quarter master at the wheel, Captain James Ferguson felt the ship buck under him like a frightened yearling. He noticed his bridge look-out, Able Seaman Angus Nelson, glance anxiously to the bow where his shipmate on look-out was facing the worst of the blow. Characteristically, Ferguson ordered the bridge look-out recalled. He knew the capabilities of his vessel, knew that she could not live in the seas ahead. But it was already too late when he gave the order to put about and return to port. The *Victoria* was just answering to the helm when she was punched amidships by a huge fist of green water, hard as malachite. Pouring over the side, flooding the decks to a depth of two feet and gathering momentum with every yard, the water pummelled the lines of cars on the ferry deck, ripped open the tarpaulin-lashed cargo trays, sending their contents spinning over the side, and finally slammed at the stern doors through which the cars were driven aboard. Burst and twisted almost off their hinges, the doors were forced back and the following sea came pouring in. At peril of their lives seamen fought to close them but the task was hopeless and the *Princess Victoria* began to list.

11.35 a.m. 'Princess Victoria To SOS'
'Position approx. five miles west-north-west from Corsewall. Car deck flooded. Very heavy list to starboard. Ship not under command.'

One of the survivors, a young Rochdale soldier, Fusilier W. Baker, described the scene:
'The doors at the back of the ship were burst open and

water poured in. Mailbags and luggage floated up. The vessel started to list and drift and we were told to put on life-jackets. We were ordered to abandon ship. Women and children were crying. Everyone tried to get into the lifeboats, on to rafts, or anything else that floated. There were sixteen others in my boat and some of the other boats were smashed. There were dozens of rafts and many people jumped into the water. As our boat was swept by heavy seas one man started praying and others in the water were praying too.'

Mr John McKnight, a cook in the vessel, took up the story:

'We had a good passage until we got to the mouth of Loch Ryan, but after we rounded the Point the cargo doors burst open. The boat started to ship water which gave us a starboard list.

At noon we had a list of 45 degrees and the rails of the ship were under water. Life-belts had been issued and the first officer broadcast to get all the people to the highest point of the deck.

At 1 p.m. there was another broadcast to say that everything that could be done had been done and the end was near. Everyone could scramble off and pick up rafts which had been floated off.

About 1.20 p.m. the ship heeled over and sank in about fifteen minutes. I jumped in a lifeboat and pushed off and endeavoured to pick up survivors. I think we got one. Subsequently I was picked up by the Donaghadee lifeboat.'

A Belfast collier skipper, Captain James Kerr, awakened in his cabin to the rumbling of lorries and cars shifting. The vessel, he was alarmed to discover, had a 20-degree list to starboard. Dressing quickly, he heard a loud speaker announcement: 'The ship is going through a crisis', and he went out on deck. He was to recall:

'There was no panic. I saw the stewards passing out life jackets from a chain. I saw one of the girl stewards named

11

Baxter, she was saying she wanted to get some ladies up.

'The list got to well over 45 degrees. There was an announcement that the ship was sinking and that a destroyer would be there in the next half hour. Soon afterwards I heard the engineer tell the captain, 'I am sorry. We are flooded. I cannot do anything.'

'It was impossible to launch the lifeboats. It was also impossible to move unless you were a bit of an athlete and had a good hand grip. In my opinion, if anyone had launched the boats in Loch Ryan I don't think many would have survived.

Then everything was happening at once. The ship was going down and I heard the siren blow "abandon ship". We had to stay put. The deckline was vertical and people were standing on the side of the ship. Some people jumped and others fell into the water.

The ship was well down in the water and coming right over gradually. When a lifeboat was washed towards the ship again, I jumped and got in. Another boat was washed under the hull of the ship and smashed to pieces.

We were very lucky. We got clear of the ship and the propellers, which were sometimes eight to ten feet in the air and sometimes six feet below the water.'

J.E. Carlin, a London civil servant, lost his wife, sister-in-law and mother-in-law. They were among twenty-six women and children drowned.

Mr Carlin got life jackets for himself and his wife. He helped his mother-in-law to put another on.

'About one o'clock I got my wife and sister-in-law on to the boat deck and went back for my mother-in-law,' he said. 'She was hysterical and resisting a little. It took fifteen to twenty minutes to get her out.

By the time I got her out, my wife and her sister had been moved along the deck. When I pulled my mother-in-law out,

12

a man gave us a helping hand because the angle of the boat was very severe. I was left hanging on to the boat rail.

There were about twenty to twenty-five women leaning against the deck-house. It seemed to me it was the obvious place for them to be, because if they had not been there, there was nothing to hold on to and the sea was not coming in there.

The men were hanging on to the rails. So far as I could see, the women were in the most favourable place.'

As Mr Carlin tried to move along the rail to get to his wife and sister-in-law, the list got worse.

He continued: 'I saw the funnel touch the water and that was the first I realised that she was going down. I was holding on to a rail which was just above my head.

Immediately below me were other women and children, but it was not feasible for me to jump down because I might have fallen on top of them. So I climbed up over the rail. I crawled along the top to try to get to my wife. As I was crawling along, the ship had turned over and I found myself on the side of the ship. By the time I got to where my wife was, she had gone.'

At the Ministry of Transport inquiry he was to claim that the other women 'most certainly slid off'.

'I think the ship went over too quickly to give much opportunity for very great help, particularly in view of the position of the women and children. They seemed to be in the best possible place at the time but, as it turned out, they were probably in the worst.

Had someone been with the women and children they might have helped.'

The group he saw on the deck must have included all the women in the ship. It would have been very difficult for any member of the crew to get along and help anybody. In fact, all the women and children on the ship were drowned.

The last hours of the doomed ship were graphically recorded in the wireless log at Portpatrick.

11.43 a.m. Destroyer *Contest* to *Princess Victoria*. Am proceeding to your assistance with all despatch. BTA 1309. Request details of extent of flooding and list. Have you power?

11.57 a.m. *Princess Victoria* to *Contest*. 35 list to starboard. Approximately twenty tons of water and cargo in car deck. Power 220 volts D.C. one hundred and twenty-three passengers, sixty crew.

12.32 p.m. *Princess Victoria* to *Contest* and GPK... Position grave but list not appreciably worsening.

12.43 p.m. *Contest* to *Princess Victoria*. Regret will not reach you until about 1330. Are you in any danger of sinking? If not, intend to pass tow on arrival and proceed to shelter of Loch Ryan.

12.47 p.m. *Princess Victoria* to GPK. Sorry radar no use. Too much list.

12.52 p.m. *Princess Victoria* to GPK. Position critical. Starboard engine room flooded.

13.07 p.m. *Princess Victoria* to *Contest*. SOS.

The *Contest* had slipped her cable at Rothesay at 11.09 a.m. on Saturday and anticipated being in the position five miles off the Scottish coast, from which the *Princess Victoria* had signalled, by 1 p.m. She had to reduce speed from 30 knots when she met the full force of the gale. Damage was done aboard and two ratings were injured, and all the time the *Princess Victoria* was drifting quickly and steadily towards the Irish coast. A wrong position signal made the *Contest* a further half an hour late at the end.

Tugs had set out from Glasgow as soon as the first SOS was sent and lifeboats at Portpatrick and Donaghadee were launched; merchant ships, a Belfast tanker and other vessels altered course to give what assistance they could.

When the coastal tanker *Pass of Drumochter* heard over her radio that the *Princess Victoria* was in difficulties, her skipper, Captain James Kelly, immediately put to sea with all speed and blew blasts on the ship's whistle to attract the attention of the master of the *Lairdsmoor*, Captain James Bell. The message was also picked up by Captain Hugh Matheson, master of the *Orchy*. The *Lairdsmoor* had a hundred head of cattle on board, and the *Orchy* was almost in ballast and very vulnerable, but Captain Bell and Captain Matheson at once put to sea. After leaving the shelter of Belfast Lough the vessels were almost overwhelmed in the very heavy seas.

The trawler *Eastcotes* was sheltering in Belfast Lough when she heard that the *Princess Victoria* was in distress. Her skipper, David Brewster, at once decided to weigh anchor and sail for the position given.

Meanwhile the stricken vessel had drifted on a south-westerly course. At 10.45 a.m., when she started to list, passengers were told to put on their life jackets. As the list increased they were ordered on to the weather deck and the captain told them over the loudspeaker: 'The ship is out of control.' Later they heard him say: 'A destroyer is coming to our assistance.'

The order 'Abandon Ship' was given and, within twelve minutes, the *Princess Victoria* sank in two hundred fathoms. She was then about five miles from the coast of County Down.

At 11 o'clock the Portpatrick lifeboat *Jeanie Speirs* was launched. The position of the *Princess Victoria* had been given in the S.O.S. message as four miles north-west of Corsewall Point and it was on this information that the Portpatrick lifeboat based her course. After reaching the position and finding nothing, she altered her course southward at 12.51

and began what was to be a long and hard search.

The Donaghadee lifeboat *Sir Samuel Kelly* was launched in a very rough sea with a full gale blowing at 1.40. At 2.02 she heard from the coastguard that the *Princess Victoria* was six miles north-east-by-north of Mew Island, but a later message gave the position farther south at five miles east of Copelands.

The Donaghadee lifeboat reached the last position given but she could find nothing. The coxswain, Hugh Nelson, decided to follow HMS *Contest*. He then heard from the SS *Orchy* that she was near survivors in a position four miles north-north-east of Mew Island. The coxswain altered course again and at 3.15 the lifeboat reached the scene of the disaster. She rescued twenty-nine people from a ship's lifeboat, one from a raft and one from another ship's lifeboat. She continued to search until five o'clock but found no other survivors and left for Donaghadee.

The Cloughey lifeboat, *Constance Calverley*, was also launched at 2.32 after receiving a message from the Tara coastguard. She made for the position given, in the teeth of a gale, and searched until six o'clock, but found nothing.

The Newcastle, Co. Down, lifeboat *William and Laura*, was launched at 4.20 at the request of the Kilkeen coastguard, but she found nothing either and reached her station again at 10.30.

The rescue of thirty-one people from the *Princess Victoria* did not end the services of the Donaghadee lifeboat that day. At 9.35 it was learnt from the Bangor coastguard that the trawler *Eastcotes* had anchored near North Briggs Buoy in Belfast Lough, and had one survivor and six dead bodies on board. At 9.45 the Donaghadee lifeboat was launched again. There was a north-by-west gale. The coxswain asked the skipper of the *Eastcotes* to weigh anchor and to go to the shelter of the Antrim coast between Whitehead and

Carrickfergus. There the lifeboat took off the survivor and the six bodies, as well as seven bags of mail that had been picked out of the sea. She then returned to Donaghadee, which she reached at 1.30 on the morning of 1 February. At seven o'clock that morning, she put out again to search for survivors with the help of aircraft in better weather and good visibility. She searched until nightfall and picked up twelve bodies and three mail bags, which were landed at Donaghadee at 7.30. The Portpatrick lifeboat returned to her station on 1 February from Donaghadee, arriving at 2.20 in the afternoon.

A plane was sent out from the RAF station at Aldergrove and another destroyer, HMS *Woodbridge Haven*, sailed from Rothesay with a doctor and medical supplies. A BOAC Constellation aircraft, flying from Prestwick to London, altered course to look for survivors and dropped a rubber dinghy to men who could be seen clinging to drifting wreckage. The *Pass of Dromochter* jettisoned her oil cargo on the seething waters.

According to survivors, there was no panic on the ship although, when the end came, she heeled over so rapidly that it was impossible to launch all the boats.

Mr E.F.W. Flack, who was rescued by the Donaghadee lifeboat, said later: 'One or two lifeboats were launched just before she went over on her side. The rest of the boats were unable to get away. There was no panic. Captain Ferguson did everything he could and remained calm as he gave his instructions.'

13.54 *Princess Victoria* to GPK. Sorry for morse OM (old man). On beam end.

13.54 GPK to *Princess Victoria*. Don't let that worry you OM.

Four minutes later Broadfoot had tapped out the last of the sixty message he sent.

SOS. Estimated Position now five miles east of Copelands, entrance Belfast Lough...SOS...SOS...SOS.

He could not know that it was the wrong position.

On the *Contest* Lieutenant Commander H.P. Fleming was faced with thirty foot waves and a water temperature of 40 degrees fahrenheit. In such a short sea he had no alternative but to reduce speed to 15 knots to prevent a capsize into the freezing sea.

At last they came alongside the *Princess Victoria* and saw the horror of the sinking. Immediately Lieutenant John McArdle of Glasgow and Petty Officer Wilfrid Warren of Portsmouth jumped overboard with ropes lashed to their bodies, acting as human grappling hooks to drag people to safety from the life rafts that bobbed in the steep sea like wafers.

Warren said later: 'Our skipper brought the *Contest* alongside and Lieutenant McArcle went overboard to manoeuvre a raft with a man on it alongside. I jumped in to help him.'

In fact, after they got the man aboard, the two sailors stayed in the freezing water for nearly half an hour, dragging a second raft with another man clinging to it alongside. This survivor told them that a woman had managed to reach the raft and hold on, but exhaustion made her let go.

When the end came Captain Ferguson made no attempt to save himself. Through the sleeting rain, survivors saw him satnding on the bridge, one had gripping the rail, the other stiffly at the salute, as the ship went down.

Said Seaman Nelson: 'Throughout all those dreadful hours the skipper was magnificent. He had the admiration of everyone on board.'

Survivors talked of the last terrifying moments before the ship sank. Steward James Blair, of Larne, said that when the order came to abandon ship some passengers had to be dragged from their cabins with lines.

'There was pandemonium for a time and it was a question of every man for himself.'

He jumped into the sea and got on to a raft and was later hauled into a lifeboat.

'While our boat was drifting some distance from where the *Victoria* went down we saw a woman on a raft. She was holding a young child and shouting for help, but we could not get near her as we had no oars.'

Eighteen-year-old Fusilier Geoffrey Bingley, of Hammersmith, said: 'It was awful to hear the cries of the people in the water. We tried to drag one or two into our lifeboat but there were no oars aboard and we couldn't reach them.'

Radio officer Broadfoot was subsequently awarded the George Cross. The citation read:

'When the *Princess Victoria* finally stopped in sight of the Irish coast, her list had increased to 45 degrees. The vessel was practically on her beam ends and the order to abandon ship was given. Thinking only of saving the lives of passengers and crew, Radio Officer Broadfoot remained in the W/T cabin, receiving and sending messages although he must have known that if he did this he had no chance of surviving. The ship finally foundered and Radio Officer Broadfoot went down with her.'

Captain James Alexander Bell, the master of the *Lairdsmoor* (Portavogie, County Down); David Brewster, the skipper of the fishing trawler *Eastcotes* (North Fleetwood); Captain James Kelly, the master of the *Pass of Drumochter* (Carnlough, County Antrim); and Captain Hugh Angus

Matheson, the master of the *Orchy* (Glasgow) were made members of the Order of the British Empire. The British Empire Medal (Civil Division) was awarded to William McConnell, the coxswain of the Portpatrick lifeboat (Stranraer), and to Hugh Nelson, the coxswain of the Donaghadee lifeboat.

The lifeboatmen also received the bronze medal of the RNLI.

The George Medal was awarded to Lieutenant-Commander McArdle and to Chief Petty Officer Wilfrid Warren. The citation stated that when the *Contest* was brought alongside the *Princess Victoria*, a survivor clinging to a raft was seen to be at the limit of his endurance, and he released his hold as the raft surged ahead in the rough water.

Lieutenant-Commander McArdle, 'without a moment's hesitation', put a lifeline around his waist, dived into the water, grabbed the man and brought him back to the ship's scrambling net. Chief Petty Officer Warren saw that Lieutenant-Commander MCArdle was having trouble and scrambled down the net. MCArdle and Warren in 'quite exceptional weather conditions' undoubtedly saved the survivor's life.

The crews of the lifeboats that went to the rescue of survivors from the *Princess Victoria* did not themselves suffer any losses. But on the same day two lifeboatmen lost their lives. They were the second coxswain and the assistant mechanic of the Islay, Inner Hebrides, lifeboat, Alexander McNeill and John McTaggart.

The Islay lifeboat *Charlotte Elizabeth* first left her moorings on 31 January at 5.45 in the afternoon. This was because of a message from the Kilchoman coastguard that a vessel was drifting and flashing distress signals three miles south of Jura. The lifeboat searched in a rough sea and a full north-north-east gale but she found nothing and reached her station again at 10.30 that night.

Soon after returning she was called out again. This was to go to the help of the trawler *Michael Griffiths*. The Barra Island, Outer Hebrides, lifeboat *Lloyds* had already gone out that morning in a full gale because of a report that the Michael Griffiths, then between seven and eight miles south of Marra Head, was full of water and had no steam. The Barra Island lifeboat and an aircraft searched widely but found nothing and the lifeboat returned to her station at 6.30.

After refuelling, the Islay lifeboat put out again at 11.50 that night. During the passage McNeill and McTaggart went down into the engine room to dry their clothes. While there, they were overcome by fumes and collapsed. The lifeboat made for Colonsay where a doctor tried to revive the two men, but one was already dead and the other died soon after. The lifeboat then returned to her station with the two dead men, arriving at 2.15 on the afternoon of 1 February. The Michael Griffiths sank with her crew of fifteen.

Among the one hundred and twenty-eight passengers and crew lost in the *Princess Victoria* disaster were Sir Walter Smiles, MP for Down North, and Major J.M. Sinclair, Deptuy Prime Minister of Northern Ireland, and all the ship's officers.

At an inquest in Belfast, the Coroner, Dr M.P. Lowe, found that the vessel shipped a quantity of water, which the scuppers were unable to clear quickly enough. More and more added to the load and the ship started to list and, shortly afterwards, was out of command.

He went on: 'The guillotine doors, which are provided as further supports to the lower half-doors against rough seas, were not down in position that day. They had not been in use for a considerable time.

If the ship had continued to drift a little longer in the same direction she was drifting, then land would have been much closer and the loss of life presumably much less.

It is my opinion that Captain Ferguson and those under him who advised the passengers to remain in the ship as long as possible did the correct thing. They knew that help was on the way and, if the Victoria kept afloat until such help came, the passengers were safer on board than in the midst of a cruel sea. The captain even went further. In the midst of his worry he kept down panic by his constant messages of reassurance that all would be well. Unfortunately, the expected aid was not to hand before the *Victoria* sank. This probably explains why no women or children were saved.

A feature at sea of which we Britishers preach is "women and children first". It is worthy of note that the captain and all his officers, with some of the crew, perished.

It is most remarkable that all those who were concerned with rescue work, either on land or sea, were not able to locate the ship's position. The destroyer, HMS *Contest*, the ships *Orchy*, *Pass of Drumochter*, and *Salvadore* were continuously looking for the *Victoria*, but at no time saw her. If the assistance of aircraft had been used earlier the *Victoria*'s position might have been located before she sank and when other means of finding her had failed.'

'I have carefully examined the chart relating to the crossing,' he continued, 'and studied the wind, sea and poor visibility on that fateful day. Such study allows for the opinion which prevailed in coastguard and lifeboat centres that the *Victoria* must drift into or close to the Scottish coast. The fact that she did not, even later on in the day, was the reason for calling the Donaghadee lifeboat into action. None can deny the bravery and hard work done by the lifeboatmen and, since Coxswain Hugh Nelson's boat was the one that landed so many survivors, let us give profuse thanks.

I would also commend the radio officer of the *Princess Victoria* who continued sending distress messages until the ship went down and, in attempting to save others, gave up his own chance of survival.'

The coroner, returning an open verdict, took as ruling the cases of the sixty-seven victims, that of Samuel Brown, aged 51, married, of Antrim Road, Belfast, who, he said, came to his death by exposure and drowning when the *Princess Victoria* perished on 31 January.

'That verdict covers all the victims,' he said.

There was more drama when a subsequent Ministry of Transport tribunal issued its 30,000-word report.

The inquiry found that the *Princess Victoria* was unseaworthy. It gave two reasons: the inadequacy of the stern doors and the inadequacy of the clearing arrangements for water on the freeboard deck. It found that the loss of life in the disaster was caused, or contributed to, by the default of the owners, the British Transport Commission, and the manager, Captain John Dudley Reed.

The report stated that they had failed to provide stern doors sufficiently strong to withstand the onslaught of heavy seas, which might reasonably be expected from time to time between Stranraer and Larne; failed to provide adequate freeing arrangements for seas which might enter the car space from any source; failed to take precautionary steps after an incident in November, 1951, when the stern doors were damaged; and failed to comply with the provisions of a section of the 1894 Merchant Shipping Act, in that they did not report this incident.

The report referred to an incident in October, 1949, when the *Princess Victoria* encountered heavy seas on the voyage to Larne while carrying milk tankers. A suggestion was made by an officer to Captain Morrow – one of the managers, assistant to Captain Reed – relative to the advisability of fitting four larger scuppers on the car deck. But this, it stated, was not done. Subsequently the stern doors were damaged and the car deck flooded off Larne but no action was taken then or at any time with regard to the fitting of extra scuppers.

'The record shows that the importance of the matter was not appreciated or, if appreciated, ignored,' stated the report. 'In November, 1951, the stern doors were damaged when the ship was travelling stern to sea. There has been an attempt made to minimise the importance of this incident . . . The court fails to comprehend why, after the 1951 incident, the necessity for stronger doors did not become a matter of urgent necessity.'

The report ended:

'If the *Princess Victoria* had been as staunch as the men who manned her, then all would have been well and this disaster would have been averted.'

Subsequently an appeal by the British Transport Commission against the Court of Inquiry's finding was dismissed by the Lord Chief Justice of Northern Ireland, Lord McDermott, subject to modifications in the findings of default. The appeal by Captain John Dudley Reed, of Pinner, Middlesex, as manager of British Railways' Irish shipping services, was allowed.

Lord McDermott said that three assessors concurred in the views and conclusions. In announcing the judgments, he changed one of the findings of the Court of Inquiry, making it read:

'The loss of the *Princess Victoria* was caused or contributed to by the default of the owners and the manager, Captain Perry (Captain H.J.B. Perry, Captain Reed's predecessor as manager), in that they were negligent before the disaster (a) in failing to appreciate that the vessel was unfit to encounter the full range of foreseeable weather conditions on the Larne and Stranraer route by reason of the inability of the stern doors to withstand heavy seas and the inadequacy of the freeing arrangements on the car deck, and (b) in not taking appropriate steps to provide adequate freeing arrangements on the said car deck, or else to make the stern doors sufficiently strong and adequate to prevent heavy seas from flooding that deck.'

Referring to a report in writing made to Captain Perry about an incident in 1951 when heavy seas damaged the stern doors and flooded the car deck of the *Princess Victoria*, Lord McDermott said that Captain Perry's reaction to the whole matter was quite clear.

'He attached no importance to the incident. He made no inquiry to find out exactly what had happened. He did not inspect the ship: he did not consider that anything had occurred which could have any bearing on her seaworthiness, and he did not report the matter to his superiors or to Lloyd's Register or the Ministry. It is most unfortunate that Captain Perry made little of this occurrence . . . His conduct amounted to default, and the finding of default against him, save in respect of the alleged breaches of statutory duty, must therefore stand.'

It must not be inferred, Lord McDermott said, that Captain Perry's default was due to indifference or carelessness of a gross kind.

And he added: 'The commission were in default as owners because they failed to discharge the Common Law duty to take due care to provide a seaworthy ship, but they were not in default because of any breach of statutory duty.'

In the Guardian on 14 September, 1979, the following report appeared:

'The owners were to blame for the unseaworthiness of a 4,500-ton freighter which sank in a North Sea storm with the loss of one of her crew, a five-day inquiry has found. The decision, announced yesterday, clears Captain Frederick Firth, master of the ship, *Hero*, and her chief officer, Mr Guy

Snowdon, of any blame.

Hero sank in a storm 90 miles from the Danish coast in November 1977. Twenty-nine crewmen were picked up. The man who died, from a heart attack and exposure, was a donkey-man-greaser Mr Ronald Elletson, aged 42, of Great Thornton Street, Hull. He died while the crew were using a life raft to abandon ship.

Yesterday, wreck commissioner Mr Richard Stone said the court's view was that the death was in part caused by water continuing to come in through the stern doors, because of their unseaworthy condition.

The unseaworthiness was caused by the wrongful act of default of the joint owners, Domino Container Ships Ltd and DFDS UK Ltd, both of London. *Hero* was a six-year-old, roll-off vessel managed by the Ellerman Wilson Line of Hull.

The inquiry's 30-page report recommends that the Department of Trade consider if cargo vessels should carry larger life rafts.'

Sources: *Report of the Ministry of Transport Inquiry into the Loss of the Princess Victoria*, published by Charles Birchall & Sons, St James St., Liverpool.

Contemporary newspaper accounts

Archives of the RNLI and Maritime Journals

Chapter Two

The Most Fortunate Fleet

The Armada was dispersed; scattered across the Atlantic like crumbs on a tablecloth.

A superb fighting machine of one hundred and thirty sail had dropped down Lisbon Sound just two short months earlier. Now it was a beaten remnant of its former vainglorious self; a few battered, tattered ships, pennants in ribbons, great sails torn to shreds, its crews fighting for their lives.

In the end the enemy had not been Drake and his long-range guns which the Armada planners had feared might prevent them from dominating Britain. It had been the weather, the worst that anyone could remember, which had been victorious over the Duke of Medina Sidonia, Don Alonso de Guzman el Bueno, Captain General of the Ocean Sea and the Armada's overall commander.

For, despite the pageantry in Lisbon Cathedral, the promises of the cohorts of priests which accompanied it and the assurances of the king who brought it into being, God was not on the side of the Armada.

Bad weather had struck at the beginning of the expedition on 9 May, 1588, when they dropped anchor inside the Belen Bar. Then they had seemed invincible. The fleet's first line had comprised two squadrons each of ten galleons, four West India men and four Neapolitan galleasses, hybrids which were half galleon, half galley.

There were forty merchantmen in the second line and thirty-four fast 'scout' ships, and twenty-three supply ships brought up the rear. In their holds they carried 123,790 cannon balls; small mountains of bacon, fish, biscuits, cheese, rice and beans; casks of wine, of vinegar and of water. No fleet was ever better victualled, its organisers believed. In a self-congratulatory way they called it *La Felicissima Armada*, the Most Fortunate Fleet.

They could not have been more wrong.

On 28 May, in line ahead formation, the Fortunate Fleet dropped down Lisbon River behind the duke in his flagship, the *San Martin*. They had already been trapped in the Sound for nearly three weeks by heavy storms and it took another forty-eight hours to make fifteen sea miles. It was another thirteen days before they reached Finistere from the Rock at Lisbon, a distance of less than one hundred sea miles. On 19 June the Spanish Fleet reached Corunna, gripped in the teeth of the worst storm of the voyage so far.

After taking on supplies – their estimate had proved woefully inaccurate and the fleet quarter masters incompetent – the Armada once more set sail. Within three days they were scattered. And when the weather abated the duke learned that two galleasses and twenty-eight other ships were missing with a total complement of six thousand sailors and marines.

Despite these losses and the duke's urgings that the Armada should be abandoned or at least deferred for another year, King Philip was adamant. The Armada must sail on. He could afford to be adamant. He was comfortably ensconced in a Spanish palace.

From the first engagement it was clear that the Armada was the least fortunate fleet in maritime history. One of the biggest Spanish ships, the *San Salvador*, contrived to blow herself out of the water and another fine galleon, the *Nuestro Senora del Rosario*, was captured by Sir Francis Drake.

But, in the end, it was the weather that defeated them and, by 13 August, the Duke of Medina Sidonia knew that he was beaten. He had lost seven first-raters and one fifth of his crews were disabled. He had sentenced twenty captains to be hanged for disobedience; his own ship, the *San Martin*, was badly holed, as were all the other fighting ships.

The duke resolved to circle Ireland and return to Corunna to refit. It was a vain hope. A month later the one hundred ships which were still afloat when the Armada reached the Orkneys were barely seaworthy. Many were wrecked on the Irish coast and at least one stately home in Wales has a magnificent fireplace in one of its state rooms made from the carved timbers of an Armada galleon which foundered off Rhyl.

Typical of the fate of many ships was that which befell the 750-ton *San Juan Baptista*, a 24-gun galleon with a crew of two hundred and forty-three. She was vice-flagship of the squadron commanded by Marcos de Aramburu, Controller and Paymaster of the Galleons of Castille.

There was little in the hulk he now commanded to suggest the grandeur that Aramburu had known. He and the remains of his crew were in a sad state. The stores the Armada had piled up in Lisbon had been unwisely distributed. Fresh food had been eaten by waiting crews as it arrived. Only the older, less palatable victuals had been stored. In fact, though it was some time before the duke was told of it, the Armada was already dangerously short of food when it sailed from Lisbon. Estimates of water had been out, too. the victuallers had assured the duke that his fleet carried enough fresh water for three or four months' supply. But on 19 June, as they tossed in their wooden walled boats off Finisterre, the Armada Council of War heard for the first time that defective water casks had resulted in the water turning green.

Now, on 11 September, her crew half starved, battle weary and exhausted, the *Baptista*, sailing only under foresail and mainsail, and the galleon *Trinidad* approached the Irish coast.

They did so reluctantly for the duke had warned them, with justice as it was to turn out, that while they would find the native population friendly enough, the English garrisons were treacherous and dangerous. But anything, it seemed, was more welcome than the wild seas that had pummelled them since Rockall. Running south-east-by-east in a thick mist with the wind abeam, it was a relief when the look-outs shouted the news of land; even though the land whose approach they were hailing was the rocky, menacing Bull and Cow Islands off the Kerry coast.

'Pilot of the Quarter Deck,' Aramburu ordered, 'lay a course out to sea and westward.'

After the islands had been identified and the first longing for an anchorage stilled, he knew his best hope was to find his fleet and head for Corunna and home.

That night and all the next day the two ships sailed line abreast into the west. With their torn masthead banners snaking in the wind, their once brightly painted fighting castles chipped and dull, they looked more like ghost ships than men-of-war.

At 5 p.m. on the 12th Aramburu consulted the glass. It had dropped sharply and beyond the bulkheads he could see the waves churned into white water. Around him he could hear the seamen talking, their muttered prayers and louder oaths. Below decks, he knew the off-duty watch was being confessed by the maritime priests.

He felt the wind blow southerly in his face and he could see that the white foam the wind had creamed was curdled now and in its place were mountainous waves of sullen blue that tossed the two ships about like beach balls in a seaside surf.

Although the two ships kept track of each other by hailing for most of the evening, by midnight, black as a monk's cowl, the *Baptista* had lost the *Trinidad*. Desperately the crew waved lanterns that spat and gutted but they saw no answering light. The *Trinidad* was lost for ever.

All that night the Baptista ploughed on, lashed by a howling gale which at daybreak veered rapidly nor-west. The sea dropped gradually and now the *Baptista* found herself driven south-east, a course she followed all day.

The morning was dismal. Though the look-out searched the horizon for hours it was noon before he saw, far away, the outlines of a large ship and a tender following. Aramburu thought it was unlikely to be an enemy ship although he must have been almost beyond caring. He ordered his ship worked down onto the distant outline and by nightfall his crew had reduced the distance between the ships to little more than a league.

But even with every inch of sail crammed on he could not approach nearer. All that night the huge lantern that hung from the stern of the galleon was kept alight and the next morning Aramburu was standing in its yellow glare before daylight taking a position. The Baptista was running south with the wind west but, to windward, the larger vessel, which Aramburu noticed was also showing a light, was heading north with the dark outline of the tender in her lee. She, too, was fleeing the dubious sanctuary of land. Yet, at daybreak, Aramburu discovered all three ships were bearing down on two large islands and on their port hand he could descry the Irish mainland. It was vital now he should identify the other ship which was getting ever closer. He shouted an order to the steering man who fought with the wheel until the galleon was facing north-north-west. Only then did Aramburu recognise the larger of the two vessels. She was the *San Juan*, 1050 tons, five hundred guns and a crewman for every gun. The *San Juan* was the vice-flagship of the Squadron of Portugal. Her commander, Don Martinez de Recalde, was Admiral of the whole Armada; even the Duke of Medina had to defer to him in matters of seamanship and navigation. If anyone could lead Aramburu to a safe haven it was he. Better yet, Aramburu recalled, Recalde knew the Kerry coast. He had commanded a squadron which landed troops at the Golden Fort in Smerwick Harbour. The land operation had been a disaster, he remembered. But Recalde had got there and, better still, found his way home again.

Aramburu knew that he could do no better than follow every movement the other galleon made. The decision was endorsed when he looked to the leeward and saw yet another Armada survivor. There was little hope for her. She was being driven by the tide and would inevitably be splintered to matchwood on the rocks of Tralee Bay.

Aboard the *San Juan*, Recalde was blessing his patron saint. Off the Orkneys he had seized a Scottish vessel and one of the crew he had taken aboard was a pilot who knew the Kerry waters even better than himself. Although the Scotsman's advice made his hair stand on end he determined that he would take it.

The islands ahead were off the Blasket Sound, the wildest stretch of a coastline, which is nowhere gentle. The seaward approach is a marrow-chilling range of breakers splintering over reefs and rocks as sharp as needles.

The course that the Scotsman was laying would mean taking the *San Juan* east, to the west of Innish Tooskent and then, still bearing east, to run before the wind to the northerly point of the second island, Carrigafadda.

The course would tax Recalde's seamanship. There was scarcely a boat's length between the two islands and the slightest misjudgment would be the end of Recalde and his crew. He, too, looked toward the mainland where the fourth Armada survivor had now struck. She had taken what was apparently the easier course and it had been her end.

He caught the mounting fear in the eyes of his crew as he

issued his orders and, as the *San Juan* lurched through the narrow channel, his own eyes were wild seeing the razor edges of the cliff face flash past, only inches, it seemed, from his face. But at last he came to a small natural harbour and with relief he ordered an anchor down.

Aramburu's ship had been standing to windward during the operation and for a time he thought that the last two months had turned his commander's head.

But, to his surprise, he too made the tricky landfall safely, followed by the tender. At last all three ships were safely anchored in the shelter of the island. Both captains were exhausted and it was not until the next morning that they met. In their relief they pressed gifts on each other. Aramburu noted in his log that day:

'Juan Martinez gave us two cables and an anchor, for we had nothing but the cable which was down, and I gave him an anchor of 30 cwt which was no use to us and of which he stood in the greatest need.'

There were, however, still problems to be resolved. On the day they had anchored Recalde had sent eight men in a long boat to reconnoitre the coast. Although he did not know it then they had been captured by English soldiers. Worried that the men had not returned, he formed a 'commando' of fifty arquebusiers and sent them ashore to find a landing place and, if possible, the missing men. They were also instructed to buy fresh meat, if they could, from any natives they might meet and to look for a source of fresh water.

They returned instead with perhaps the one piece of news the Spaniards would have given their ships not to have heard.

Firstly, they reported, a landing was impossible. There were steep cliffs all round the island. But worse news was to follow. On top of one of the cliffs they had seen a party of a hundred arqubusiers waving a flat of a red cross on a white ground. English troops, plainly.

Martinez knew that he was safe while he lay at anchor but, for the three days the Spaniards sheltered under the island, they were only able to collect small quantities of fresh water as it ran down the cliffs. Things were even worse for Aramburu. All his ships' boats had been torn away in the storms of the preceeding weeks so he was unable to send any water parties ashore.

On the 21st, after three calm days at the anchorage, a westerly blew up with such violence that the *San Juan*'s anchor cable snapped as though it were sewing thread. To Aramburu's alarm she started to drift down on the *Baptista* which lay directly in her path. There was nothing Aramburu and his crew could do. They had to watch helplessly as the *San Juan* began a race to get another anchor down before the two galleons locked. They were too late. The two ships smashed together and the great stern lantern of the *Baptista* came crashing down on the deck, to be followed shortly by the mizzen mast tackle. Fortunately the *San Juan*'s anchor at last bit and held; only moments had saved the two ships from damaging each other beyond repair.

The two crews had barely recoverd their senses when they were rivetted by the hollow boom of a cannon from the north-west. As one man they turned towards the sound and the sight which met their eyes was one that symbolised the death of the Fortunate Fleet.

From the north-west, drawn by the land, came what looked to Aramburu like the skeleton of a great galleon. Her sails, saving only her foresail, were in tatters and a single cannon, mounted in her bow, boomed intermittently a distress signal.

Aramburu recognised her as the *Santa Maria de la Rosa*, 943 tons, vice-flagship of the Guipuscia squadron.

Slowly she sailed up the narrow channel and, as she came

under the shelter of the cliffs, her crew let go her last anchor. For a while it appeared that she might be safe but at 2 p.m. the incessant beating of the tide against her stern became too much and on the turn she began to drift towards the *Baptista*. Aramburu had barely time to register alarm before he realised that he, too, was drifting until only two cable lengths separated the two ships.

He wrote: 'In an instant we saw that she was going to the bottom while trying to hoist the foresail.'

She sank in seconds.

'Immediately,' he wrote, 'she went down with the whole crew, not a soul escaping – a most extraordinary and terrible occurrence.'

In fact, out of the two hundred and ninety-seven ship's company, one man did survive. He was the pilot's son, Antonio de Morana. He floated ashore on some wreckage and was taken to Dingle where he was questioned by the authorities. The answers he gave still tantalise treasure hunters. For after he had listed the grandees who were aboard, her fifty great cannon, twenty-five pieces of brass and cast iron and fifty tons of sack, he claimed that fifty thousand golden ducats, as much again in silver and a king's ransom in gold and silver plate went down with her. Marine archaeologists believe that her remains – and her treasure – lie off Stromboli Rock in two and a half fathoms at low water.

When the underwater rocks ripped the bottom out of the *Santa Maria* it was a warning to Aramburu. They, too, were drifting onto the same rocks and all they had to hold them off was an old anchor with a broken stock. The stock had been repaired and fitted to the cable Martinez had given them. Their first anchor had given way and they put out the second, makeshift one hoping it would hold long enough to enable them to haul in the first anchor, inspect and repair it.

Mercifully, the second anchor held and the *Baptista*'s head came round. They could concentrate for a little while on the other. When it was hauled in Aramburu saw that only the stock and part of the anchor remained, the rest had been snapped off and the cable was badly chafed where it had rubbed against the rocks. The damage had obviously been done when the *Baptista* had dragged in the ebb tide.

While the crew worked on repairs Aramburu's attention was diverted as yet another Armada ship limped into the anchorage. She, too, was named the *San Juan* and she was in an even worse case than her namesake. Without a boat to send, Aramburu could only look on helplessly as the mainmast gave and a sudden gust of wind blew her fores'l – all the canvas she still had – to threads. But her captain, Fernando Horra, was a fine seaman and, as men on the other ships watched, he let go his anchor and brought the hulk to.

The next morning when Don Martinez heard of the condition of the *San Juan* he ordered her crew to be taken aboard by Aramburu and the captain of the tender. After her stores had been shared she was fired and blazed most of the day until at last she sank at her moorings.

Aramburu was anxious to return to Spain but Don Martinez was shipping the guns from Horra's vessel and refused to be hurried. However, he gave Aramburu formal permission to return and the *Baptista*, its crew rested and increased, set sail on the morning of 23 September with a light easterly wind.

They had barely sailed two cables before the wind dropped and they found themselves being drawn by currents into the rocks of the island they had just quitted. Luckily the wind revived and, with top gallants set, the *Baptista* once again headed for the open sea. However, the wind dropped once more as they reached Blasket Sound and the vessel began to drift onto the rocks, pulled this time by the tide.

They had only one spring. It held until an hour after nightfall when yet another wind blew up, this time from the south-east, setting them once more adrift.

Among the equipment Aramburu had rescued from the *San Juan* before she was fired was a small boat. It was launched and, though the seas threatened to engulf them, the sailors in it managed to catch a line thrown from the prow of the galleon and pulled her round on the single spring.

The anchor weighed, the *Baptista* set sail. Aramburu had to lay a course in the pitch dark that would take them windward of reefs but, instead, he found himself drawn back toward the islands. There was nothing else for it. He would have to negotiate the difficult passage between the islands. In violent rain, with a heavy sea running and vision limited by thick cloud, it was even more daunting than their first attempt, but it was successful. Aramburu noted afterwards in his log:

'It pleased Our Lady, to whom we commended ourselves, that we should get out, sailing all that night to the west so that by morning we found ourselves eight leagues from land.'

But not out of danger. Three hours after daylight a violent storm with high seas and driving rain hit the galleon. For two hours the frightened sailors fought to keep the galleon afloat. At last the storm abated and the crew began to bring the *Baptista* about in order to lay to. They had barely begun before anothe great storm blew up and the galleon began to pitch and roll alarmingly. The *Baptista* was in no condition to ride such a sea; her masts strained against the deck housing, snapping the rigging thread and forcing open the oakum-and-pitch-caulked deck seams. The wind had barely dropped before the tired crew were put to caulking, sewing and splicing. It was evening before sailing orders were given but by dawn the next day they were clear of the islands, three leagues out to sea in calm weather.

The next day in a south-east-by-south they tacked to the west and, doubling Dorsey Head, at last put the land between themselves and their original anchorage. By the 26th they were ten leagues out to sea. Even when the wind chopped round west-south-west the vessel sailed on under press of canvas. On the 28th there was yet another change of wind. A south-south-west had been blowing all day but at night a north-west gale whipped up and the foresail disintegrated under the force.

In the teeth of the gale all hands were mustered to haul in the main topsail but they were unable to fold it in the high wind.

Wrote Aramburu:

'The ship began to roll tremendously, in consequence of which the guns which were with the ballast shifted to port with the barrels and cables and three seas struck us in the waist so that we thought all was up with us. We got up a studding sail on the foretackle, commending ourselves to God and His Blessed Mother. With this, the ship began to get fairly under control. And so we remained for what was left of the night until the morning.'

In the morning the wind began to drop perceptibly, the sail makers were able to put in order an old foresail, while the rest of the crew worked at righting the ship. By the 30th they had got the topmast up and were getting the galleon shipshape . . . And that night they faced yet another gale.

Wrote Aramburu: 'Till morning we sailed south without getting the topsail set as it looked like bad weather and, owing to the sickly state of the crew, there would have been trouble in case it had been necessary to take in sail.'

Recalde brought his ship into Corunna on 7 October. He had set sail with the tender which he turned into a hospital ship. Unable to keep up and in order to get help for the casualties, her captain took her up the Channel and ran her aground on the Devon coast.

His patients fared better than their compatriots who were washed up on the Irish coast. Although the Irish population did what they could to hide them, those who were captured by the 2,000-strong English garrison were murdered on the orders of the Lieutenant Deputy, Sir William FitzWilliam.

Of the magnificent fleet of one hundred and thirty vessels which had set sail, only 44 ships returned to Lisbon. Among them was the *San Juan Baptista*.

Sources: *The Defeat of the Spanish Armada* by
          Garret Mattingly
          Armada Ships on the Kerry Coast by the Rev. W.S.
          Green, C.B., N.A. (Proceedings of the Royal Irish
          Academy, February 1901)

Chapter 3

Lifeboat Rescues

Between 1994 and 1998 Welsh lifeboats were launched four thousand five hundred times, their crews saved a thousand lives and helped three thousand three hundred stricken boaters and seamen.

The lifeboat service calls for a special bravery. It is hard enough to be a hero when disaster overtakes you at sea. But a special kind of bravery is needed to stand on a safe shore and launch yourself into a wild sea where every moment may be your last. Even today, when lifeboat crews are protected by the latest high tech equipment, it still takes great courage to accept a jacket and climb aboard a lifeboat when the maroons go up.

On the Isle of Anglesey, where the lifeboat service was pioneered, this heroic tradition goes back a long way and includes three rescues that were classics of their kind . . .

The skipper of an American sailing ship called them the 'Straits of Hell' and Coxswain William Owen remembered the description as he stood behind the wheel of the steam lifeboat *Duke of Northumberland* fighting the tide rip beyond Holyhead harbour.

A sailor since boyhood, Owen knew of no more frightening stretch of water than 'The Race' where the seven-mile-an-hour current is lashed by gales and the sea becomes a cauldron of spume and wild water. He had never known it as deadly as it was on that morning, 22 February, 1908.

The west-south-westerly gale was gusting at more than 80 m.p.h. Outside the harbour the seas were awesome. Owen had been a lifeboatman for forty-three years, the last twenty as coxswain. As a boy, he remembered being taken to see the wreck of the *Royal Charter* at Moelfre in which four hundred and fifty-one passengers and crew had perished after the gale that had claimed her. The great iron steamship, *Great Eastern*, had been in Holyhead then and she had all but sunk at her morrings. Mostly though he remembered his personal tragedy. He had lost a son in a sailing boat in Holyhead harbour. And when he told the story you could hear the mixture of puzzlement and pride in his voice:

'She was going out on a life-saving errand,' he recalled. 'I was in the sailing lifeboat then and she passed us. We were just slipping our moorings when I saw her pass in the night and I heard my lad's last hail.

From that time to the present I have never seen him nor his body for he was never found. All I can suppose is that the boat carried too much sail and was driven under. There were five men in the boat and all were lost . . . '

As the *Duke* ploughed on the coxswain remembered other losses. Just beyond the bend in the breakwater the sailing ship *Cuba* had smashed into the stone, bows on, and she had been ripped to pieces before the lifeboat could reach her. Everyone aboard had perished and the cox remembered the most poignant incident of all. The bodies of three-year-old twins had been washed up seven miles down the coast. Despite the seas which had torn at them and the rocks on which it had finally thrown them, there had not been a mark on their bodies. When Owen saw them they reminded him of two wax dolls.

He felt the power of the *Duke* surge under his feet. She was the marvel of her day. She had no screws; her propulsion came from water forced through tubes in her hull. She could never be entangled in wreckage and it took her only minutes to build up a head of steam. There had been services, thirty years past, which might have ended differently had the *Duke* been on the station. In one week two ships had been lost before the pulling and sailing boats could reach them. But there had been others . . .

Once when Owen had been repairing his nets in the attic of his cottage his son, a child then, had called him to see the pretty red rockets in the sky. A distress signal, obviously, but by the time Owen reached the window they were dying sparks in the distance.

At the station, when he raised the alarm, the other lifeboatmen were reluctant to believe him. But Owen could read the name on a ship's bows at two miles' distance.

'Launch the boat,' he advised. 'It was a distress signal.'

Still unconvinced, the crew climbed into their 'waistcoats', the lifeboat was launched and they pulled on their oars in the direction that Owen had seen the red sparks of a dying rocket. As they pulled they reminded him how easy it was to confuse signals at sea at night.

Owen was to recall: 'I was certain I was right. I always pinned my faith on my son. The weather was bad that night, but not too bad for clear seeing.'

Sure enough, after the crew had been pulling on the great oars for nearly an hour, they came upon the wreck. She was a Swedish ship, which had capsized. Her keel was pointing skywards and her crew were clinging desperately wherever they could find a hand-hold. It was only when they had been handed into the lifeboat and brought to safety that the Swedes learned what a narrow escape they had.

The rocket that Owen's son saw was the only one they had time to fire before the ship had rolled over in the heavy seas. Had the boy not called out, had Owen not reached the attic window in time and had his eyes not been sharp enough to identify the dying sparks, there would have been no survivors.

Memories like these crowded in as the *Duke of*

Northumberland built up steam. The 'pullers and sailers' would be no use this day, Owen told himself. This was the second time that morning that the *Duke of Northumberland* had been called out. They had launched shortly after noon to the aid of the steamer *Bencroy* from Liverpool. Heavy seas were carrying her onto the breakwater. From the shore, watchers cried their distress. The *Bencroy* had put out two anchors but no one on shore believed they would hold over such a ground and in such a gale. It could only be moments before she struck and within a very short space smashed to tinder. For the big seas had her now and she was pitching and rolling her way to certain destruction.

The watchers saw the funnel of the lifeboat sticking out of the waves like a bookmark as she rounded the breakwater. Perhaps there was a chance now. As one man, the watchers began to pray, eyes open. They were seamen; they wanted to see the struggle which was unfolding beyond the breakwater.

The *Duke* reached the steamer; two lifeboatmen were winched aboard. Sliding on the storm-washed decks, they soon had a hawser made fast and thrown to a second steamer which, until now, had been standing helplessly by. The rescue steamer billowed smoke, the tow braced taut and slowly the *Bencroy* was drawn to safety.

Less than an hour later the lifeboat had launched a second time.

A tiny coaster, the *Harold*, had fired distress rockets. Another Liverpool vessel with a crew of nine, she was hopelessly under-powered and she, too, was being carried to destruction on the rocks.

The weather had worsened disastrously in the brief hour since the last service. There was a howling, bitterly cold gale and the crew were drenched and smothered by huge seas. They were hardly making any way at all. Even under the

Duke's power it took nearly two hours to get out of the harbour and round the breakwater. At any time the deck crew could have been swept over the side. Battened below decks, the engineers, should the *Duke* capsize, would have been trapped like rats in a cage.

The Race was a foaming cauldron. The roar of wind and sea was deafening. The lifeboat was tossed about like an empty rum keg. Even if she reached the *Harold* there was every chance she would be smashed against her side by the pitching sea.

Owen ordered drogues out to steady the *Duke* on her course. It was a mistake. Though they steadied her they reduced her power, drawing her back onto the rocks. There was only one chance. Signalling for the drogue to be brought inboard and for more power from the engine room, Owen made a breakneck dash for the *Harold*. Once alongside, he had to take the *Duke* right round her hull before he found a place to board her. When he found it on the starboard hand as they were borne by a huge wave, he hailed the skipper and told him to pay out a string rope so they could tie up alongside. The rope was thrown and caught. No sooner was it made fast than it snapped and the *Duke of Northumberland* was swept away on a heavy swell. When they were carried back by the next swell Owen hailed the skipper for the second time.

'Another rope. And from the same place.' He paused. 'We can do nothing without one. If you don't give us one you will be utterly lost.'

A second rope was thrown, made fast on the lifeboat and a bosun's chair improvised. One by one, seven crewmen came swinging across to the safety of the *Duke of Northumberland*. An eighth was just preparing to follow when an immense sea broke over the lifeboat from the north hand. Owen felt the deck lifting under his feet as the *Duke* was

44

carried on the wave. They must be carried over the *Harold*'s deck, he thought, and drowned or smashed to pulp against her broad side. Between them the two vessels carried thirteen fenders but they would have been no use against such an impact.

A second mountain of water struck the lifeboat. At first it carried them head-on towards the *Harold* but then it slackened and they felt themselves sailing past her stern. The two vessels were almost touching and for the remaining two crewmen it was the final chance. There would be no opportunity now of rigging a bosun's chair. Their only chance was to leap from the deck and hope that they landed on the deck of the lifeboat.

They launched themselves at the moment the *Duke* was swept broadside along the starboard hand and, by the grace of God, both men landed on her deck to be swept up and carried to the warmth of the fore-cabin.

The rescue won for William Owen the RNLI's gold medal, the lifeboatman's VC, to be worn with the silver medal he already held. That was presented to him by the future King George V, on the 4 May, 1908, when he was still Prince of Wales and President of the RNLI, in a ceremony at Marlborough House.

The citation described Owen's action as one of 'exceptional merit attended by grave risk to all on board the lifeboat which would certainly have ended disastrously had it not been for the gallant and extremely skilful management of the lifeboat by Coxswain Owen.'

The Prince of Wales was interested in the engineering of the steam lifeboat and Owen did his best to explain the principles. He also told the Prince that, within twelve hours, the seas had reduced the abandoned coaster to matchwood. In a burst of confidence he added:

'It seemed as if the Almighty had just hurled us up to the

broadside to get those last two sailors off the wreck. For I believe that God has always given a big hand with me whenever I put to sea to save men's lives.'

What Coxswain Owen did not tell the Prince of Wales was that, rather than undergo another investiture, he would gladly have faced two more such rescues. He admitted to a friend: 'I was scared stiff.'

* * *

A later Holyhead lifeboat was involved in the most dramatic rescue of modern times. This also involved the Moelfre boat and ended with the unprecedented award of two gold medals.

The S.S. *Nafsiporos*, a Greek coaster, had been storm-bound off Ramsey Head for two days when, on 2 November, 1966, she began to drag her anchor and was soon drifting crabwise over huge seas in a gale that was gusting at 100 m.p.h.

Her skipper, Angelo Katsovufis, was only 28 and the ship was his first command. He was on the bridge with his first mate, Evangelos Pittas, only a year older than himself, when the Chief Engineer John Patsoulas reported that the screws were lifting clear of the water and, as a result, the engines were overheating.

At 8.20 a.m. the *Nafsiporos*'s distress signals, giving her position as twelve miles south of Douglas Bay, were picked up and the Douglas lifeboat, the 46-ft. R.A. *Colby Cobbin No. 1*, was launched. But with visibility at 500 yards there was little hope that Coxswain Richard Lee could find her.

At 9.50 a.m. the Ramsey coastguard reported she had drifted eleven and a half miles. An hour later she was spotted by a Shackleton from RAF Kinloss 25 miles off Douglas Head. At that time Coxswain Lee estimated he was within five and a half miles of her. But though he searched all day in these terrifying seas he could not find the steamer. Finally, at 6.30 p.m and only when his fuel was dangerously low, he reluctantly returned to station.

In Holyhead, the lifeboat station had been warned that the *Nafsiporos* had been sighted out of control 20 miles off Point Lynas, Anglesey. Unfortunately, all telephone wires had been blown down in the gale which had also rendered the maroons useless. Lt. Commander Harold Harvey, the RNLI Inspector of Lifeboats who was visiting the station, agreed to make up one of the scratch crew which Coxswain Tom Alcock, a former bowman at Rhyl and only three months in his new command, was trying to form.

At 10.30 the *St Cybi*, a 52-ft. Barnett Class lifeboat, was launched into a north-west gale, Force 10, gusting to Force 11.

The *St Cybi* searched for three hours before, at 1.30 p.m., she made contact with the Shackleton, which led her to the Greek steamer.

Steaming to her aid, too, was a Russian timber ship, the *Kingurley*. She was already trying to get a tow aboard but it was proving difficult. The *Nafsiporos* was yawing 60 degrees port and starboard and most of her crew had been injured in falls. A tow was made fast but it parted after 25 minutes.

At 1.55 p.m. the coastguards asked the Moelfre lifeboat, the *Watkin Williams*, whose coxswain was Richard Evans, to join the search.

Although the Moelfre crew had been out on service in heavy seas since 7.40 a.m., they returned to the station at once and, at 1.55 p.m., launched for the second time.

The *Nafsiporos* was outside the Moelfre patrol area. With only a vague idea of the passage, her radio smashed by a 32-ft. wave, there was no way of getting to the charts below decks because of the danger of flooding the boat, Coxswain

Evans had no illusions about the danger his crew faced. At one point the deck ventilators were ripped away by a wave and the sea poured into the bow under the foredeck, pulling her down at the prow. At the hazard of their lives, the second cox, Murley Francis, and a crewman, Coxswain Evans' son David, scrambled forward and plugged the holes in the deck with spare life jackets.

The *St Cybi* arrived on the scene of the drama at the same time as a rescue helicopter from RAF Valley, the Anglesey air sea rescue station. The helicopter tried to winch a crewman down to lift the Greek mariners off but the turbulence was so great that the pilot had to abandon the attempt.

The *St Cybi* tried next, sweeping round the stern of the steamer only to be hurled back by a monster wave.

The *Watkin Williams* arrived just as the *St Cybi* was being swept away. The tide was ebbing strongly east to west and twice the *Watkin Williams* rode in on it from the west. But the Greeks refused to jump despite the frantic signs from the lifeboat.

By this time the *Nafsiporos* was lying in five fathoms of water less than a quarter of a mile to the west of the rocky East Mouse island. Battered by the 100 m.p.h. gale and the 35-ft. high waves, she was yawing 35 degrees to port. A lifeboat, which had become entangled as she was being lowered, swung from her davits like a pendulum.

Tom Alcock on the *St Cybi* realised that only a highly experienced bowman could hope to snatch the seamen to safety from the swinging lifeboat and, even then, only at the risk of his life. He decided to take the job on himself and, calling Commander Harvey to take over the helm, he scrambled up the foredeck with his second cox, William Jones.

Harvey meanwhile lay down the *St Cybi* to hit the steamer beam-on at the jumping ladder in the waist, from which he could observe seamen hanging. As they hit the side so they were lifted 20 feet up, enabling Alcock and Jones to grab five Greeks and throw them into the lifeboat. The last one had just landed safely when the ship's boat finally broke free from the davit. Alcock and Jones barely had time to jump clear before it crashed onto the foredeck where they had been standing.

The impact smashed the *St Cybi*'s radio mast and a pair of oars crashing through the wheelhouse window narrowly missed Harvey's head.

Next to go in was the Moelfre boat. A beam wave hit her as she came up on the jumping ladder but Francis and Evans were able to pull ten more Greeks aboard.

Both lifeboats, by coincidence, had senior officers aboard. An ex-Naval Commander in the *St Cybi* and, in the *Watkin Williams*, Captain David Jeavons who had been master of six Canadian Pacific deep sea vessels and was on leave before going to to command the *Empress of England*.

Both paid tribute to the volunteer crews with whom they served.

Said Captain Jeavons:

'The men on the deck on the port side of both lifeboats took terrible risks. The *Nafsiporos* and the lifeboats were roaring towards each other which meant that the men on the port side risked being totally crushed. The Greek seamen were reluctant to leave and had to be literally dragged off the side. This meant that the men on deck were on the port side for a long time taking risks. Personally I was amidships catching the bodies as they were thrown across and I was not in much danger. I was therefore able to observe the risks the other men were taking . . . the engineers were absolutely terrific. The remarkable response from the engine rooms – instructions had to be shouted over the noise of the wind and sea – undoubtedly saved the day.

49

'The sea and weather were certainly not what deep sea men would call boating weather. To call conditions extreme is really an understatement and I was truly impressed by the strength of the lifeboat.'

Her young skipper and four of the crew had stayed aboard the *Nafsiporos* throughout the storm. The following day the steamer herself was towed to Liverpool by the tug *Utrecht*.

A month later Commander Harvey and Cox'n Richard Evans were awarded gold medals; Coxswain Alcock and Eric Jones and Evan Owen, the engineers of the boats, won silver medals; every other member of both crews was awarded a bronze medal.

* * *

For crewman Hugh Owens, the *Hindlea* service had been the second time he had taken part in an historic rescue in the Moelfre boat. As a boy on 28 October, 1927, he had been a member of the crew in the epic service to the coaler *Excel* which got into difficulties off Carmel head in passage from Liverpool to Holyhead. On that night Richard Evans' uncle William Roberts was second coxswain and, in the absence of the cox, commanded the crew.

The Moelfre boat was the first of nine to be launched, five from North Wales and four of them from Anglesey. Apart from the Moelfre pulling and sailing boat, they included the motor lifeboat from Beaumaris, the steam lifeboat and a second puller and sailer from Holyhead.

A whole gale was blowing when the maroons went up and the boats were launched into an icy, heavy sea. It took the crew two and a half hours to find the ketch in a helpless condition, made fast to a German steamer. As the lifeboat approached the steamer cut the tow rope to the ketch and sailed off. The ketch fell off to leeward as the Moelfre men made a vain attempt to get alongside. She was already waterlogged and it was obvious a rescue attempt had to be made at once if its crew were to be saved.

Sailing with the crew was a Captain Jones, a blue water skipper and a local with unrivalled knowledge of these coastal waters, but not a crew man.

Roberts and Jones decided to take the lifeboat under full sail across the deck of the *Excel*. They knew that the odds were against them and that they were almost certain to damage, even to wreck, the lifeboat. But they did not hesitate. The heavy sea lifted the lifeboat on to the *Excel*'s upper deck. She was stove in three places, two on the port side and another, very much larger, on the starboard side. The three man crew of the *Excel* were hauled aboard and the lifeboat was swept off by a second monstrous wave just as the ketch floundered. The German steamer made no attempt to aid them.

The lifeboat was still in great danger. Her hull was badly damaged and she was so full of water that, instead of riding the seas, she cut through them. Her jib was blown into ribbons, severely impairing her ability to sail, but she struggled towards the Menai Strait, beating against the wind. She reached it by 2 a.m. and anchored off Puffin Island having sailed between 15 and 20 miles. It was during this passage that a member of her crew, another William Roberts, died of exposure. One of the ketch's crew was severely injured and soon after died. In the pitch dark with a full gale blowing, no one knew how he had been injured or even when he died.

At Beaumaris the lifeboat was on standby but shortly after 6 p.m. both phone and telegraph broke down and the Cox was stationed in the boathouse to watch for signals. Just before 10 p.m., amidst growing alarm that the Moelfre lifeboat had not returned, Beaumaris launched. In towering seas she made for Linas Point, cruised towards the Menai roads and then returned to the Strait where she found the Moelfre boat moored. Due to what the RNLI subsequently described as 'an unfortunate misunderstanding' the Beaumaris crew thought the Moelfre crew were in no need of help and returned to station.

The Moelfre lifeboat with her exhausted crew remained at anchor until daylight where she was seen from Beaumaris. The lifeboat was launched for a second time and brought her under tow to their station. Ashore, the Moelfre crew were taken to the Bulkeley Arms. They had been at sea for seventeen hours, during which time second cox Roberts did not once leave the tiller. For some hours after he landed he was completely blind, from the salt water, the wind and the terrible strain of unceasing watching. Whilst he was at the tiller, command was shared between him and Captain Jones. Both were awarded gold medals. The rest of the crew were given bronze medals and a pension was awarded to the widow of William Roberts with a special allowance for their dependant grandchild. The Moelfre Hon. Sec. Colonel Lawrence Williams was awarded an inscribed barometer. To keep in touch with his boat and to keep up communications after the island's phone and telegraph wires were blown down he was out in his motor car all night. His citation read:

'He had narrow escapes from falling trees and visited many places in the course of the night that are considered dangerous for a car even in daylight and did not return home until he knew the boat was safe.'

Another barometer went to the Hon. Sec. of the Anglesey boats, Captain R.R. Davies, who, like the colonel, had been out in his car all night.

Meanwhile, at Porthdinllaen on the other side of Caernarfon Bay, two steamers were seen making distress signals. The gale was blowing so hard that the Hon. Sec. Captain Owen Evans and the cox – unnamed in the official report – had to crawl to the boat-house to avoid being blown over the cliff.

The Porthdinllaen boat had a link with the earliest lifeboat on Anglesey. In 1870 the Rev. Owen Lloyd Williams, already the Hon. Sec. of the Abersoch Lifeboat Service, added Porthdinllaen to his command. He was the son of the Rev. James Williams – an ancestor, incidentally, of the distinguished painter Sir Kyffin Williams – who founded the Anglesey Life Saving Association in 1828. He had served as a crewman on the Cemlyn lifeboat, winning a silver medal for a service where he took command of the lifeboat.

The history of the Trearddur Bay lifeboat since it was first launched in 1967 is less dramatic than its older sister station on Anglesey but it is one of the busiest, covering the whole of the island's west coast.

Its 15-foot inflatable, *Gemini*, was involved in a dramatic rescue on 2 September, 1971, when it was called out to assist a sailing dinghy capsized beyond 'Cod Rocks'.

In a heavy swell and a Force 6 sou' wester, one of the dinghy's crew was hauled inboard but the other was swept over the knife edge rocks. Whilst helmsman John Burns kept the ILB head to sea, crewman Mike Williams got the second man aboard. By this time a huge sea had built up, exposing rocks below and astern of the boat. Burns opened the throttle wide, the ILB breasted a wave, jumped clear out of the water and exposed rocks and made for its base at Porth Diana. Both men were awarded Bronze Medals.

Since 1967 the Beaumaris station's inshore inflatable *Atlantic 21* has been supplied by the BBC children's programme *Blue Peter*.

Its crew have won six silver and a bronze medal. The most

recent bronze was awarded to Coxswain David Gallatin in 1981 for rescuing the crew of two of the fishing vessel *Wygir*. In a 70-knot gale, with the lifeboat screen coated with heavy snow and ice, a tow rope to the *Wygir* broke. Gallatin decided he must take the two man crew off. With superb seamanship he slowly brought the boat round, head up into the wind, hauling a second tow rope inboard, bringing the fishing boat to the lifeboat's stern. As she came alongside, the *Wygir* rolled heavily, damaging the lifeboat's fender and guard rails. The *Wygir* was being driven astern and then back up the lifeboat's port quarter. The two fishermen had just time to jump aboard before she was driven onto rocks and broke up.

* * *

Hugh Jones, the first coxswain of the Llandudno lifeboat station in 1861, was a copper miner. When there was a service call it was the duty of his daughter to rush to the top of the shaft, halfway up the great Orme, and rap out an SOS with a stone on the side of the shaft which brought her father rushing to the service.

The station has saved two hundred and thirty-seven lives at sea but its greatest moment came on land in February 1990 when its crew were one of three – the others were Rhyl and Flint – which saved five hundred and eighty in the Towyn Floods which followed the breach of the sea wall in hurricane force winds and exceptionally high tides.

Using the inflatable and its high clearance launching vehicle in difficult, dangerous and extremely uncomfortable circumstances, families and their pets were snatched from the flood waters. Some lifeboatmen spent up to 19 hours in the freezing water.

Meurig Davies, the Llandudno cox, recalled: 'There was

such a force of water that manhole covers were being lifted. You just had to tread gingerly.'

Flint lifeboatman Terry Jacklin recalled: 'The fire chief was warning everybody about the street lights. It hadn't crossed my mind that under the water the street lights might have been live.'

During the Second World War the Pwllheli and Barmouth lifeboats were largely engaged in rescuing the crews of crashed planes, some from the RAF camp *'Owen Glendower'* on the site of what is now a holiday camp.

Alas, none were able to better the signal sent to Lloyds by the local coastguards when the Porthmadog schooner *Twelve Apostles* ran aground in 1898: 'Twelve Apostles Making Water in Hell's Mouth.'

Down the coast in South Wales tragedy struck twice at Mumbles lifeboat station. On 27 January, 1883, whilst attempting to rescue the crew of a German barque, the lifeboat was thrown violently against her and was swept over successive ridges of rocks by heavy seas. Four of the crew, including the two sons of the Coxswain Jenkin Jenkins, lost their lives. Then on 1 February, 1903, the lifeboat capsized off the entrance to Port Talbot harbour with the loss of six of the fourteen man crew.

It was around the same position on 11 October, 1944, that the coxswain William J. Gammon won a gold medal and bronze medals were awarded to mechanic W.G. Davies and Bowman Thomas J. Ace. They rescued the crew of forty-two of the Canadian frigate *Cheboque*, smothered in heavy seas on the Bar. Twelve times in darkness and heavy squalls the cox brought the lifeboat round through the surf alongside the frigate so the men could jump to safety.

Three years earlier Gammon and his mechanic Robert T.

Williams won bronze medals for their part in the rescue of the crew of ten of the steamer *Cornish Rose*, dragging her anchor in Swansea Bay.

In 1947 tragedy struck Mumbles for the third time. Gammon and W.G. Davies were among the crew of eight lost when their lifeboat *Edward Prince of Wales* capsized during a rescue off Sker Point.

A lifeboat was named in his honour and sixteen years later the *William Gammon* was involved in a service as dangerous as any in the history of the station.

At 8 p.m. on Sunday, 17 November, 1963, the motor vessel *Kilo of Amsterdam* reported a fire in her deck cargo of sodium drums. There had been heavy explosions but the ship radioed she was not in immediate danger and was making for Swansea.

Maroons were fired at the Padstow station at 9.55 and half an hour later the lifeboat, *Joseph Hiram Chadwick*, one of the 52-ft. Barnett class, slipped her moorings. A south-westerly gale was blowing, gusting to storm force 10, and the sea was exceedingly rough. There was fierce rain with hail squalls and visibility was poor. It was one hour before low water.

Coxswain John Murt steered to the north-west in the hope of intercepting the *Kilo*, but at 11.12 a message was received that the *Kilo's* position was 14 miles from Lundy Island. It was clear the Padstow lifeboat was engaged in a fruitless chase. She was recalled at 11.45 and reached her station at 2.45 the next morning.

Meanwhile a decision had also been taken to launch the Tenby lifeboat. Maroons were fired at 12.40 and ten minutes later the Tenby boat, *Henry Comber Brown*, a 46-ft. Watson class, was launched. Coxswain W.R. Thomas set a course towards the Helwick light vessel.

As the lifeboat cleared the lee at Caldey Island, the wind increased to storm force and the waves were twenty to twenty-five feet in height. A very heavy sea broke on board, carrying away the canvas screen doors of the wheelhouse and buckling the after cabin door.

In the early hours of the morning a third lifeboat was launched. This was the Mumbles boat, *William Gammon – Manchester and District XXX*. Maroons were fired at 2.48 but there was such a severe thunderstorm that some of the crew did not hear them. With the help of the police, Captain Mock, the secretary, succeeded in contacting the crew, and the lifeboat, another 46-ft. Watson, was launched at 3.20. About the time of launching, the Mumbles coastguard recorded a maximum wind speed of 64 knots.

Coxswain Thomas, in command of the Tenby lifeboat, realised that he had little chance of catching up with the *Kilo* unless she were stopped or slowed down by another explosion. A Shackleton aircraft of the Royal Air Force was flying over the *Kilo* and dropping flares but, although the coxswain could see the flares, he could not pick out the casualty. At 4.07 he learnt that the Mumbles lifeboat had sighted the *Kilo*, but he decided to press on in the hope that he might be able to give some assistance.

The Mumbles lifeboat also had an extremely severe passage. Waves were over twenty feet high and at times the Mumbles light was hidden by the spray.

It was at 4.07 that Coxswain Lionel Scott, in command of the Mumbles lifeboat, first sighted the *Kilo* in the light of flares dropped by the Shackleton. He estimated that he must be about half a mile off. The Dutch vessel was a mass of flames and there was fire over the sea ahead and downwind of her.

Coxswain Scott made his first run in at 4.11. A heavy sea threw the lifeboat under the *Kilo*'s counter and he was forced to overshoot. He made a second run, but the *Kilo* sheered heavily to starboard and shipped a heavy sea. This caused the deck cargo to explode in a mass of flames. At that moment the lifeboat surged towards the burning well deck of the *Kilo* and it was only by quick and correct use of the helm and engines that Coxswain Scott was able to keep the lifeboat clear.

Coxswain Scott began to manoeuvre for a third run in but the flames then died down and the master of the *Kilo* decided not to abandon ship but to make for the Mumbles. About 4.50 the *Kilo* beached in Mumbles Bay with the lifeboat alongside her port quarter. The Swansea pilot vessel *Seamark*, which was equipped with fire-fighting apparatus, was also standing by but she could not help as any water directed on the burning sodium would only have fanned the flames.

After about three quarters of an hour the fire aboard the *Kilo* increased again. It started to spread to the holds, which contained whisky, grease and acetone, and there were further explosions. The master, believing the ship was now in serious danger of blowing up, decided his crew should be taken off. There was another sudden burst of flame. Coxswain Scott had to back off and return to lie alongside the *Kilo*'s stern. The *Kilo*'s crew were sheltering aft and they were all taken off successfully by the Mumbles lifeboat.

Meanwhile the Tenby lifeboat was in some difficulty with trouble in the oil pump of the port engine. Coxswain Thomas, knowing that the *Kilo* was being escorted into Mumbles Bay by the Mumbles lifeboat, decided to make for Swansea. By 6.20 the lifeboat was in Mumbles Road and at 8.15 she secured in Swansea south dock.

When the tide made a turn, the *Kilo* was seen to refloat and Coxswain Scott volunteered to put some of the *Kilo*'s crew aboard to let go an anchor but the master decided that the risk of an explosion was too great.

The torrential rain continued and there was a thunderstorm and, by 6.30, the fire on board the *Kilo* had begun to die down. The pilot vessel Seamark managed as a result to get a line aboard and to begin towing. The *Kilo*'s master then asked Coxswain Scott to put him and his chief engineer back on board.

The *Kilo* was able to move under her own power and she was berthed in Swansea Dock at 7.55. At 8.12 the Mumbles lifeboat landed the remainder of the *Kilo*'s crew at Swansea Dock. Some idea of the weather conditions may be gained from the fact that the coxswain had to use the drogue while entering the lock.

For this service the silver medal for gallantry was awarded to Coxswain Lionel Derek Scott of the Mumbles. The thanks of the Institution, inscribed on vellum, were accorded to the other eight members of the Mumbles crew: Second Coxswain W. Davies; Motor Mechanic R. Gammon; Assistant Mechanic W. Tucker; Signalman J. Bailey; K. Kostromin; W. Parsons; T. Randall; J. Whitford. Letters of appreciation were sent through the honorary secretaries to the crews of the Padstow and Tenby lifeboats.

After his heroism during the *Kilo* rescue Coxswain Scott was in action again on 3 October, 1968. He won a bronze medal when he and his crew rescued seven men from a dredger that ran aground on the Trusker Rock near Porthcawl.

On 12 April, 1971, this indefatigable man took a dinghy out on an ebb tide to rescue a boy, Alun Bessette, who was being swept out to sea clinging to an upturned boat. Scott first saw Alun in the tide race off Mumbles Head. The sea was short and steep with ten foot waves and the boy was plainly exhausted.

Scott launched a dinghy but had difficulty handling it in the confusing and unpredictable sea. Several times he had to throw himself forward to prevent the dinghy from being tipped bow over stern; all the time maintaining a precarious balance to prevent capsize. When he reached Alun, the boy was too exhausted to haul himself aboard the dinghy.

Scott tied him to the dinghy while he removed the engine to clear a space to bring him inboard. His own strength failing, Scott could only lift the boy when the dinghy stern sank in the trough of a wave and both he and Alun were thrown backwards by the impetus of the lift. By this time there was nine inches of water in the dinghy but Scott made it back to the edge of the race where he was met by the Mumbles ILB, which had been alerted by Mrs Scott. Scott was awarded a bar to his silver medal.

Youngsters and sea water is a dangerous mixture. In her admirable book, Shipwrecks of Wales (Carreg Gwalch £3.50), Dilys Gater tells of two tragedies.

The first was at Aberdyfi on 27 February, 1839, where the crew of the brig *Favourite* invited three teenage pupils from Mrs Scott's Boarding School for Young Ladies at Penhelig to join them aboard for a farewell supper before they sailed. Also invited was 17-year-old Ann Felix, daughter of the licensee of the Britannia Inn where the girls had arranged to meet the crew.

The girls were not missed from school for three hours. A boat was sent to the *Favourite*. She was deserted, the table still laid for an uneaten supper. Subsequently the ship's boat was found wrecked at the mouth of the estuary. The bodies of the party who had sailed in her were washed up on beaches over a distance of several miles.

In Tywyn churchyard you can still see the tombstone to Ann with its heart rending epitaph, written and carved by her heartbroken father:

Weep not for me, my parents dear,
I am not dead but sleeping here.
Prepare, prepare to follow me

You cannot prepare too soon
For the night did come
Before I thought it noon.

It was a grim prophecy. Within a year Ann's mother died unable to bear her sorrow.

Caernarfon Bay was the scene of a wreck and an attempt at rescue which was subsequently the subject of a sermon preached in Westminster Abbey.

On 13 October, 1881, in a full gale one of the engines of the MV *Cyprian* burst, the steam steering gear failed and finally water swamped the furnace, firing the single remaining engine. When the port anchor was dropped it ran away with its chain. Captain John Alexander Strachan ordered the crew to don life jackets and prepare to abandon ship. It was at that moment that a stowaway, J.W. Khalan, crept on deck.

Realising there were no life jackets for the boy, Captain Strachan took off his own and gave it to him. 'I'll swim,' he said.

The captain and eighteen members of the crew were drowned when the *Cyprian* struck two miles off Porth Dinllaen. The stowaway was one of only eight who survived.

Sources: *The Quiver*, 1909
             Shipwrecks of Anglesey and the Lleyn by
             Ian Skidmore
             RNLI archives
             RNLI *Historic Shipwrecks of Wales*

Chapter Four

Rescue

Bravery is the basic coinage of the RNLI and its crews spend it without heed. Not only on the Welsh coast. The Irish coast is every bit as treacherous as the Welsh, and in bad weather Welsh crews would be the first to acknowledge the bravery of their Irish comrades. Here are a few of their stories of gallantry.

The Kilmore Quay lifeboat was launched at 1.50 a.m. on Chirstmas Eve, 1977, into a rough sea with a west-south-west wind, Force 8-9, and moderate visibility after a report by Wexford Garda that four red flares had been sighted off Bannow Bay. There were no breaking seas but the lifeboat was kept at half speed because of the swell and the spray. After a search of two hours with no results, Coxswain Thomas Walsh radioed he would continue searching on his way back and turned for Kilmore Quay at about 4 a.m.

The Kilmore Quay lifeboat *Lady Murphy*, which was built in 1972, is one of twenty-six boats of the 37-ft. Oakley self-righting class in the RNLI's fleet. The type which rights herself after a capsize by a system of transference of water ballast, was designed by Mr Richard Oakley, a former naval architect to the RNLI. Following the disaster in 1970 when all except one of the crew of the Fraserburgh lifeboat lost their lives following a capsize, the RNLI undertook to give all offshore lifeboats a self-righting capability by 1980. Since 1958, when the first self-righting Oakley lifeboat came into service, lifeboats of this class have been launched over 1,750 times and have saved more than nine hundred lives.

As the *Lady Murphy* neared the shore Walsh noticed that sea conditions had worsened. About one mile south-south-west from Forlorne Point the lifeboat was hit by a very high breaking sea on the starboard side, capsizing her to port. When she righted the coxswain, Joe Maddock, was missing. Acting mechanic John Devereux restarted both engines without any trouble and the boat was turned back to the south-west – to starboard – with Dermot Culleton and his brother David manning the searchlight. Two or three minutes later Maddock was heard shouting to starboard and was picked up in the light of the searchlight. He was pulled aboard over the starboard side forward by Dermot Culleton, Finto Sinnott, John Devereux and the coxswain.

When Walsh examined the damage caused by the capsize he found that part of the windscreen was shattered and the mast broken. The drogue had streamed itself and the coxswain had the drogue ropes made fast.

Maddock was placed in the forward well and Dermot Culleton and Finto Sinnot, who had a badly cut head, stayed with him.

Walsh was by this time unsure of his position. Harbour and street lights were not working and he found it difficult to judge the distance off. He decided to continue to the south-east, at slow speed, and then turn north to enter the harbour. But, as the *Lady Murphy* turned north, a second heavy breaking sea hit her on her port beam, capsizing her for the second time to starboard, but this time hurling four members of the crew into the sea.

The three men left aboard were the coxswain, John Devereux and crewman Eugene Kehoe. The lifeboat was still heading towards the harbour but was being set rapidly down to the eastward towards a dangerous shoal called St Patrick's Bridge. Crewman David Culleton was in the water close by the stern. The coxswain and John Devereux pulled him aboard and then went forward to pull in Dermot Culleton who was hanging on to a grab line on the starboard bow. Joe Maddock could be seen just to the west but he was subsequently washed alongside.

The lifeboat was now setting down towards the broken water of St Patrick's Bridge. Calling for three of his crew to hold on to Joe Maddock, Walsh returned to the wheel to alter course to clear the breakers. The three men had great difficulty in holding Joe Maddock alongside as the lifeboat gathered way but managed to keep their grip and, a few minutes later, he was brought aboard into the dorward well, suffering badly from exposure. Only Finto Sinnott was missing now and Walsh searched the area further, looking for him until he was back abeam the harbour. There was no sign of him and Walsh, concerned about the state of the rest of his crew, had no alternative but to halt the search and return to Kilmore Quay. Rather than turn across the weather, he stemmed the seas and tide and allowed the lifeboat to crab towards the harbour entrance before turning in.

Second coxswain John Connick and the station mechanic, Liam Culleton, who had not been aboard for the service, volunteered to take the *Lady Murphy* out again at daylight with a new crew to search for the missing men. An army helicopter and the Rosslare Harbour lifeboat were also called to go out and search from the east but at 10.10 Finto Sinnott's body was found washed up on the beach.

A team of two RNLI inspectors flew to Ireland the same day. They decided the most likely case of the abnormal seas which overwhelmed the lifeboat on both occasions was the refraction of the heavy swell in the shoal conditions off Forlorne Point, which was accentuated by the tidal stream. This caused a build-up of the sea and a number of exceptionally large breaking waves to occur in the area. A former lifeboat coxswain, Kim Bates, reported waves breaking over the harbour wall and estimated their height as 30 feet; the watchman of the Coningbeg light vessel described the seas, with a wave height of 30 feet, as the worst he had seen in 20 years, and waves at Tuskar Rock lighthouse were 20 feet, the worst the keeper had seen for six years.

The inspectors reported that Coxswain Walsh's action in picking up Joe Maddock after the first capsize was a 'tribute to his leadership and determination'. Their report continued 'that he was able to rescue three of the four men in the water after the second capsize and take the lifeboat safely into harbour is indeed remarkable . . . his physical strength, personal courage and determination saved a major loss of life.'

They went on: 'Acting mechanic John Devereux also fully contributed to the rescue of Joe Maddock and the other two men. His courage and determination played an important part in saving their lives.'

The inspector also praised the second coxswain and his crew for taking out the lifeboat at daylight to further search for the missing man.

An RNLI Committee of Management investigation subsequently found that ' . . . a contributory cause of the loss of life of Finto Sinnott was that the deceased had discarded his life jacket after the first capsize. Another factor was probably his shocked condition due to a head injury received during the first capsize.'

It was the first capsize on service of a self-righting lifeboat but the investigation decided that 'there was no error of judgment by the coxswain nor failure of the lifeboat or its equipment which contributed to the capsizes' and that 'the lifeboat was overwhelmed by a heavy breaking sea on both occasions.'

For his leadership, determination and exceptional courage in recovering members of his crew and bringing the lifeboat back to her station, Coxswain Walsh was awarded the RNLI's silver medal for gallantry. Acting mechanic

Devereux was awarded a bronze medal. The tanks of the RNLI inscribed on vellum were awarded to the other members of the Kilmore Quay crew, Maddock (acting second coxswain), Culleton (acting assistant mechanic), Culleton and Kehoe (crew members). A special posthumous vellum went to Sinnott's widow who also received an RNLI pension.

A gale was blowing from the south-east with a very heavy sea, sleet and rain when the Cloughey, County Down, lifeboat, *Herbert John*, was launched to rescue the crew of a steamer gone ashore half a mile off Ballyquinton on 21 January, 1942. As she was launching, another message came from the coastguard to warn the coxswain that the steamer was in a very rocky part and to say that the coastguard life-saving apparatus was also going to her help. When the lifeboat reached the steamer at 3.30 a.m. she was high on the rocks. It was impossible for the lifeboat to get near her but, for the present, her crew was safe. The coxswain intended to stand by but he saw ships to the north, evidently part of a convoy, off course and heading towards the shore. He went towards them at once but found that several had already struck and two others were about to strike. The lifeboat flashed her lamp and a destroyer, which was also heading inshore, put up star rockets. When she saw by their light that it was a lifeboat signalling, she turned and headed out to sea towards the rest of the convoy.

Seven ships had by this time gone on to the rocks, too far inshore for the lifeboat to give them any help. At daybreak she went to each of the ships to see which required help. The tide had ebbed and, except for one, they had been left high and dry and their crews appeared to be in no danger. One ship only was in sufficient water for the lifeboat to get to her. She was the *Orminster*, of London, with sixty-eight on board. An attempt to refloat the steamer failed. The captain at first allowed some of his crew to go aboard the lifeboat but afterwards ordered them to return, with the exception of two who remained on the lifeboat. The lifeboat returned to her station at five that afternoon.

Three-quarters of an hour after the Cloughey lifeboat had been called out, the neighbouring Newcastle crew and launchers were assembled. Three hours later the coastguard rang up the station to report the grounded ships off Ballyquinton Point and at 5.05 the motor lifeboat, *L.P. and St Helen*, cleared the harbour. She had a journey of over twenty miles in a very strong south-south-east gale. A rough sea was running and the night was very dark with rain and sleet. Sometimes the coxswain could see for half a mile, at other times less than the length of the boat.

The lifeboat had to cross the Strangford Bar, where a nine-knot tide was running out against the gale, making a mass of jumbled seas, breaking in every direction. Once into this tideway, the cox went with it, steaming out against the gale, dodging the seas, and at every opportunity edging the boat out to the north. He had to steam against the gale in this way for six miles and it took him over an hour to clear the bar. Then, with his drogue out, he made his way back towards the land. Day was now beginning to break.

At 10.30 he reached the scene and found not four but seven ships ashore. Six were close inshore but one of them, the *Browning*, of Liverpool, was lying farther out with her stern on a reef of rocks. She was the vessel the Cloughey lifeboat had offered to help but her captain did not wish to be taken off. Since then the lifesaving apparatus had rescued from the shore seventeen of the fifty-six men who were on board but, to get near enough to work their apparatus, the men had had to scramble out on to the rocks. The tide was rising and, by the time they had rescued those seventeen men, it had risen to their shoulders. It drove them back and they could rescue no more. On board the steamer were a number of horses, bloodstock stallions. They had gone wild with fear and had broken loose. The captain had had to give orders for them to be shot and, in the confusion, the seaman who did it put two bullets through his own hand.

When the Newcastle lifeboat arrived she anchored to windward of the steamer and tried to drop down to her on her cable. But the gale was now blowing its hardest and the seas were breaking right over her. To go alongside was like trying to go alongside a breakwater. At one moment the lifeboat was lifted by the seas as high as the steamer's rail; but for the cable she would have been flung on her deck. The next she was caught in their backwash and whirled away. Three times the coxswain dropped anchor and attempted to go alongside but after an hour he had to give it up as impossible. He then hailed the steamer and asked if there was any water on the lee side where the lifeboat could float. he steamer's captain answered that there was. But the steamer's bow was very close to rocks and the lifeboat would have to go by the narrow channel between the two. The coxswain laid her for that channel, waited for his moment and called on his mechanic for full speed. At its widest the channel was little more than twenty feet; at its narrowest sixteen. The lifeboat was nearly nine feet broad. But he brought her through unscathed into a lagoon of calm water under the steamer's lee.

He soon took off twenty-nine of the steamer's crew, one more than the number which this type of lifeboat is supposed to carry in rough weather, but there were still ten men on board the steamer. The coxswain knew the risk that he would run in taking them. They would add three-quarters of a ton for the lifeboat to carry which would bring her deck almost awash. In that overloaded boat he would have many miles to travel. At the same time he knew that it would be impossible to return. He accepted the risk and took them.

Some of the rescued men were far spent and they were huddled away wherever they could be packed. At the coxswain's request, the captain told all who could to lie down and to lie still. The lagoon where the lifeboat lay under the steamer's lee was so small that there was no room to turn her and it was impossible to go out stern first through the narrow channel between the bow and the rocks. The only other way was to take the lifeboat right across the reef on which the steamer's stern lay. It was a most hazardous thing to attempt, for between the seas there was very little water on the reef. Had any mistake been made in crossing it the lifeboat would have stranded, the next wave would have capsized her, and all on board would have been thrown into the sea. The coxswain chose his time well. He was lucky enough to get three big seas one after the other. Then he put the boat at full speed and crossed the reef without touching it. No one on board knew what he intended and, when the mate of the *Browning* saw what he had done, he said, had he known, he would never have left the wreck.

The lifeboat had crossed the reef but she was still not out of danger. Newcastle was twenty miles away and it was impossible to return there against the gale with the overloaded boat. Instead, the coxswain ran northwards before the gale, through unfamiliar waters, feeling his way, for he could see little, among rocks and reefs. He had the drogue out all the time to keep the overloaded boat steady before the heavy following sea and his rail was often rolling right under.

At 2.30 in the afternoon, nine hours after setting out from Newcastle, he brought the lifeboat safely into the harbour of the small fishing village of Portravogie. There the rescued men were landed. Six were sent at once to hospital twelve miles away. The rest were taken in by the villagers. The lifeboat could not return to her station against the gale and her crew went home by road. They arrived at 10.30 that night, exhausted and wet to the skin. Two days later, when the gale had moderated, they returned to Portavogie for the lifeboat.

It was a service of the greatest hazards in which the coxswain showed reckless daring, great coolness and superb seamanship. The RNLI made the following awards:

To Coxswain Patrick Murphy, the gold medal for conspicuous gallantry, with a copy of the vote inscribed on vellum. He was also awarded the British Empire Medal.

To Second Coxswain William Murphy and the motor mechanic Robert Agnew, the silver medal for gallantry, with a copy of the vote inscribed on vellum.

To William J. Lenaghan, bowman, Thomas McClelland, assistant motor mechanic, and Patrick McClelland and Patrick Rooney, lifeboatmen, the bronze medal for gallantry, with a copy of the vote inscribed on vellum.

* * *

On Friday, 7 February, 1936, a gale from the south-east sprang up on the south coast of Ireland with a very heavy sea. The gale increased until, about midnight on Monday the 10th, it was blowing a hurricane force never before experienced by the oldest inhabitant in Ballycotton. Huge waves were smashing over the pier and breakwater. The harbour was a seething cauldron. At high water on the Monday evening nothing could be seen of the breakwater or the pier. Stones, a ton in weight, were being torn from the quay and flung about like sugar lumps.

During the Sunday and early on Monday the coxswain, Patrick Sliney, ran ropes from the lifeboat, the *Mary Stanford*, a 51-ft. Barnett cabin motor lifeboat, to prevent her from striking the breakwater. At midnight on the Monday, when the gale had risen to a hurricane, the coxswain's own motor boat was seen to have parted her moorings and was in danger of being carried out to sea. The coxswain and several other men attempted to launch a boat to her but were nearly swamped. They succeeded at last and got a rope to the motor boat and secured her. It was at that moment, after a long, anxious night, that a call came for the lifeboat. The Daunt Rock Lightship, with eight men on board, had broken from her moorings twelve miles away and was drifting towards Ballycotton.

Seas were breaking over the lifeboat house where the boarding gear was kept. The Secretary, Robert H. Mahony, did not believe it possible for the coxswain even to get aboard the lifeboat at her moorings. 'I was afraid to order him out,' he admitted afterwards.

Sliney went down to the harbour. A little later the lifeboat was at the harbour mouth, dashing out between the piers.

Said Mr Mahony: 'The coxswain had not waited for orders. His crew were already at the harbour. He had not fired the maroons for he did not want to alarm the village. Without a word they had slipped away. As I watched the lifeboat I thought every minute that she must turn back. At one moment a sea crashed on her; at the next she was standing on her heel. But she went on.'

People watching left the quay to go to the church to pray. A mile off, at the lighthouse, she met seas so mountainous that their spray was flying over the lantern 196 feet high. Then the lifeboat hesitated and turned round. The watchers thought she was coming back but the coxswain took her through the sound between the two islands. It was more dangerous than the open sea but it would save half a mile.

Through the sound the seas were tremendous. The lifeboat came off the top of one sea and dropped into the trough of the next with such a terrible thud that everyone thought the engines had gone through the bottom of the boat.

Quipped mechanic Mick Walsh: 'All's well. After that she will go through anything.'

The coxswain ordered the whole crew in the after cockpit and, after each sea had filled it, he counted his men.

The lifeboat drove safely through the sound and ran before the wind along the coast. Off Ballycroneen, about six miles from Ballycotton, the following seas got worse and Sliney decided to put out his drogue to steady the lifeboat. As he eased the engines to, several seas struck him on the head, half stunning him. Then, as the drogue was being put out, an extra heavy curling sea came over the port quarter, filling the cockpit and knocking down every man on board. When they had recovered they found the drogue ropes had fouled but the drogue was drawing.

The lifeboat ran on towards the shore but, in the spray and rain and sleet, the shore was not visible and nothing of the lightship could be seen. He decided to make for the usual position of the lightship and put the lifeboat's head to sea. He went on for seven miles until he came to what he thought her position had been but, owing to the erratic course he had taken, and in the rain and sleet, he could not be sure. He decided to run for Queenstown for information. He had no drogue to steady the lifeboat in the breaking seas in the mouth of the harbour and had to use oil sprays to calm the breakers.

After he got the position of the lightship from the pilots at Queenstown, he put to sea again and, just after midday, he found the lightship. She had got an anchor down a quarter of a mile south-west of the Daunt Rock and half a mile from the shore. H.M. Destroyer *Tenedos* and the S.S. *Innisfallen* were standing by her. When the lifeboat arrived the *Innisfallen* left. The crew of the light vessel did not want to leave her. They knew the danger it was to navigation that the lightship was out of position but they feared their anchor would not hold and asked the lifeboat to stand by. It was too bad to anchor but she kept slowly steaming and drifting.

About 3.30, when the gale had eased a little, the *Tenedos* anchored to windward of the lightship, dropped down towards her and tried to flat a grass line to her with a buoy attached in order to get a wire cable to her and take her in tow. When this failed the lifeboat picked up the buoy and got close enought to the lightship to pass it to her. It parted before they could get the wire cable attached to it.

The *Tenedos* now got under way and came closer to the lightship. The lifeboat again passed the grass line to her. This time she got the towing wire on board but the wire parted. These attempts had taken nearly two hours and the *Tenedos*, the lifeboat and the lightship had been continually swept by heavy seas. It was now dark and impossible to make another attempt to get the lightship in tow. As the *Tenedos* was going to stand by all night, Sliney decided to make for Queenstown for more ropes and food. His crew were wet through and exhausted, they had not eaten since the night before and had been up all that night trying to save their boats.

The lifeboat reached Queenstown at 9.30 p.m. Mr Mahony had already tried to get through to Queenstown. Appalling road conditions prevented him getting more than half way but, when he reached the coxswain by telephone and learned the position, he returned at once to Ballycotton and set out for Queenstown with spare drogue, drogue rope, tripping line and veering lines, and changes of underclothing for the crew. It was 23 miles to Queenstown and, again, a very difficult journey by night, dodging fallen trees. He arrived at Queenstown at three in the morning of Wednesday the 12th.

Some of the crew had managed to get a little sleep but all the time there were three men on call in the lifeboat. Early in the morning of the 12th, the lifeboat set out again. As soon as she reached the lightship, H.M.S *Tenedos* left, but the Isolda, the vessel of the Irish Lights, was expected from Dublin. The wind dropped a little during this, the second day, and fog set in. But the sea did not go down and the lifeboat stood by all day and all that night.

At daylight on the 13th, shortly after seven, the coxswain decided to make again for Queenstown as his petrol was getting low. When she reached Queenstown at nine on that morning she had been standing by for twenty-five and a half hours with the seas breaking continually over her crew who had also not eaten.

At Ballycotton Mr Mahony had one hundred and sixty gallons of petrol ready but it was impossible to get a motor lorry. He telephoned to Cork to send eighty gallons but the driver of the lorry injured his arm and a second driver had to be found. The lifeboat had the petrol on board and set out again at four in the afternoon.

When she reached the light vessel again, about dusk, she found that the *Isolda* had arrived. Her captain told the coxswain that he intended to stand by all night and in the morning would try to take the lightship in tow. But the weather since four o'clock had been getting worse. At eight o'clock a big sea went over the lightship, carrying away the forward of the two red lights which are hoisted by a lightship at bow and stern to show that she is out of position. At 9.30, with the wind and sea still increasing, the coxswain took the lifeboat round the lightship's stern with his searchlight playing on her. In its light he could see her crew, with their life belts on and the seas breaking over them, huddled at the stern. The wind, which had been south-east, had gone to south-south-east. The lightship was now, the coxswain estimated, not more than sixty yards from the Daunt Rock. He went to the *Isolda* and told her captain that the lightship

74

was now in great danger. She was very near the rock. She was to the south-west of it. The wind was shifting. If it went a bit west she must strike the rock.

The captain said that in the heavy sea it was impossible for the *Isolda* to do anything. The coxswain asked if he should try to take the crew off. He was told to carry on. He took the lifeboat round the lightship again. The seas were going right over her. She was plunging tremendously on her cable, rolling from 30 to 40 degrees, burying her starboard bow in the water and throwing her stern all over the place. She was fitted with chocks, which projected over two feet from her sides, and, as she rolled, these threshed the water.

To anchor to windward and drop down to her was impossible owing to her cable. The only thing was to get astern and make quick runs in on her port side, calling on her crew to jump for the lifeboat as they could. The coxswain went within hailing distance and told the lightship's crew what he intended to do. He must run in at full speed, check for a second, then go full speed astern. In that second, the men must jump. He knew the dangers. The lightship was only 98 feet long. If he ran too far, the lifeboat would go over her cable and be capsized. As he came alongside, the lightship, with her chocks thrashing the water as she plunged and rolled, might crash over right on top of the lifeboat.

The coxswain went ahead of the lightship, pumped out oil to calm the seas a little – but the tide was running strongly and the effect of the oil did not last long – went astern of her and then drove full speed alongside. One man jumped, and the lifeboat went astern. A second time she raced in but no one jumped; a third time, and five men jumped; a fourth time – the lightship sheered violently and her counter crashed on top of the lifeboat, smashing the rails and damaging the fender and deck. No one was hurt but the man working the searchlight sprang clear only just in time. The lifeboat went in a fifth time. Again no one jumped.

There were still two men on board the light vessel. They were clinging to the rails. They seemed unable to jump. The coxswain sent some of his crew forward, at the risk of being swept overboard, with orders to seize the two men as the lifeboat came alongside. Then he raced in for the sixth time. The men were seized and dragged in. As the coxswain said, it was no time for 'by your leave'. One of the men had his face knocked against either the fluke of the anchor or a stanchion and badly cut. The other man's legs were hurt. The motor mechanic was able, with iodine and bandages, to give first aid to the man whose face was cut. Shortly after the rescue one of the men of the light vessel – the long strain on them had been tremendous – became hysterical and two men had to hold him down to prevent anyone from being hurt or knocked overboard.

The lifeboat, after reporting to the *Isolda*, made for Queenstown, where she arrived at eleven on the night of 13 February, and the two injured men were taken to hospital. The lifeboat remained at Queenstown for the night, returning next morning to Ballycotton where she arrived at 12.45 p.m. She had then been away from her station for seventy-six and a half hours.

She had been out on service for sixty-three hours and she had been at sea for forty-nine hours. During the first and third days the weather was bitterly cold and the rain and sleet almost continuous and, during the whole time, the lifeboat was taking heavy seas on board.

All her crew came back suffering from colds and salt-water burns, and the coxswain from a poisoned arm. All were completely exhausted. In the sixty-three hours from the time when they left Ballycotton until the time when they brought the rescued men into Queenstown they had had only three hours's sleep.

The RNLI made the following awards for this exhausting service.

To Coxswain Patrick Sliney, the gold medal which is given only for conspicuous gallantry, and a copy of the vote of the medal inscribed on vellum and framed.

To each of the four members of the crew, Michael C. Walsh, Thomas F. Walsh, John S. Sliney and William Sliney, the bronze medal and a copy of the vote of the medal inscribed on vellum and framed.

To Mr R. H. Mahony, honorary secretary of the station, an inscribed binocular glass.

* * *

Early on the morning of 27 November, 1954, the 20,125-ton Liberian tanker *World Concord*, in ballast and bound from Liverpool to Syria, broke in two during storms of exceptional violence in the Celtic Sea.

None of the members of the crew was near the point where the break took place. Seven men, including the master, were in the fore part, 35 men were aft.

The first ship to answer the *World Concord*'s SOS was the aircraft carrier HMS *Illustrious*. The St David's lifeboat, *Civil Service No. 6*, was launched at 8.28. A moderate gale was blowing from the west, there were fierce rain squalls and the sky was overcast. Visibility was about one mile. At 9.15 the *Illustrious* signalled the lifeboat that the *World Concord* was fifteen miles north-north-west of the South Bishop Lighthouse. The lifeboat reached the after part of the tanker at 11.45.

By this time a fresh gale was blowing from the south and there was continuous heavy rain, with waves reaching fifteen to twenty feet in height, and a long and powerful swell. The tanker was rolling heavily, her propellers turning all the time.

The coxswain, Captain William Watts Williams, decided to make a dummy run in on the starboard to discover the best way of taking the men off the stern half of the tanker which then lay athwart wind. After making this run he asked for the Jacob's ladder to be shifted to the well deck forward of the break of the poop. In this way a shorter length of ladder would be needed and the confused water around the stern could be more easily avoided.

The coxswain stationed five men forward in the lifeboat and came alongside the Jacob's ladder which had been re-rigged as he had asked. He took off the first survivor and the lifeboat went slowly ahead, and then astern, until she was abreast of the tanker's propellers. This manoeuvre had to be repeated thirty-four times, one survivor being embarked each time. The rescue took fifty minutes and the survivors, who were thirty-four Greeks and one Egyptian, none of whom could speak English, were all taken on board without injury.

By the time the lifeboat left the *World Concord* at about 12.30 the weather had grown much worse. Visibility had decreased to half a mile and a whole gale was now blowing from the south. Through heavy seas the coxswain brought the lifeboat through the northern entrance of Ramsey Sound and reached the slipway about three o'clock. The seas were such that rehousing was a difficult operation and the survivors could not be landed for more than a quarter of an hour.

Meanwhile, the fore part of the *World Concord* had continued to drift, with seven men on board. At 1.30 on the afternoon of 27 November the Rosslare Harbour lifeboat was asked to help.

A severe south-westerly gale had been blowing in St

George's Channel since the day before. The seas had been so heavy that the Fishguard-Rosslare mail steamer had taken six hours instead of the scheduled three hours and fifteen minutes for the crossing. Weather conditions in the southern Celtic Sea were the worst for many years. Despite this, the Rosslare lifeboat, *Douglas Hyde*, was launched at 3.50 and reached the tanker's position at 7.10.

Coxswain Richard Walsh had to decide whether to try to take the survivors off at once or to wait until daylight. It seemed that the fore part of the tanker was in no immediate danger, and he decided that the risk would be greater if he tried to take the survivors off in darkness. His decision meant that the lifeboat would have to stand by for twelve hours in terrible conditions. During the long wait Coxswain Walsh shared the wheel with Second Coxswain William Duggan. It was extremely difficult to keep sight of the tanker. She showed no lights and was drifting northwards at about three and a half knots. About midnight the wind reached full gale force from the west-south-west.

The next morning, at 8.30, Coxswain Walsh decided that the time had come to take off the seven survivors. The tanker's fore part was then running before the wind and sea. She was listing about five degrees to port. There was a heavy swell and seas sometimes reached twenty-five feet in height.

Coxswain Walsh made two dummy runs to the south on the starboard side of what remained of the *World Concord*. Then he came alongside about half way, keeping the lifeboat clear of broken and protruding parts of the tanker.

By manoeuvring the engines, he kept the lifeboat alongside the 25-ft. jumping ladder. In fifteen minutes the remaining seven men, including the master, had been taken on board the lifeboat which suffered only slight damage.

The coxswain believed himself to be rather further south than he was but he later altered course and, at two o'clock in the afternoon, an aircraft chartered for press purposes indicated the course to Holyhead. About three o'clock the lifeboat met the Holyhead lifeboat, which had been launched shortly before, and the two boats returned to Holyhead at 3.30 in the afternoon. By that time the Rosslare Harbour lifeboat had been nearly twenty-six hours at sea.

For their services the RNLI made the following awards:

Silver Medal:Coxswain William Watts Williams of St David's and Coxswain Richard Walsh of Rosslare Harbour.

Bronze Medal: Motor Mechanic George Jordan and Assistant Motor Mechanic Gwilym Davies of St David's and Second Coxswain William Duggan and Motor Mechanic Richard Hickey of Rosslare Harbour.

Thanks of the Institution inscribed on vellum: Assistant Motor Mechanic John Wickham, Bowman James Walsh, Lifeboatman Richard Duggan, Lifeboatman John Duggan, of Rosslare. Second Coxswain David Lewis, Acting Bowman William Rowlands, Lifeboatman William Morris, Lifeboatman Howell Roberts, Lifeboatman Richard Chisholm, of St David's.

Sources: RNLI archives

Chapter Five

Three Men in a Boat

The nineteenth century produced a special breed of man: the scientific adventurer, the engineer with the creative imagination of a poet.

The Revd George William Garrett, B. A., was just such a man. The son of a poor Manchester vicar, he was put to Rossall School at the expense of the great Victorian philanthropist, Baroness Burdett Coutts, and went on to become a member of the first chemistry class at Manchester Grammar School. He was a prodigy of scholarship. At Trinity College, Dublin, he passed his first year examination within a week of joining the class. At the age of 17 he was appointed an assistant master at the Manchester Mechanics Institute. In his spare time he won proficiency certificates in Science, Art, Physical Geography, Geology, Higher Mathematics and Higher Chemistry. While studying for his B.A. at the South Kensington Museum, in the fashion of the day, he read theology and was ordained by the Bishop of Manchester. He became a competent navigator by making a voyage round the world. And he had a secret dream. He wanted to invent the first workable submarine.

There had been submersibles long before his time. The first drawings for a submersible craft were sketched in the 16th century by Leonardo da Vinci; the first designs were made in 1578. But it was not until 1801 that the first serious attempts to make an underwater craft were made.

Robert Fulton, an American jeweller turned engineer, had settled in Paris in 1799. Two years later Napoleon awarded him a grant of 10,000 grancs to build a submarine. The result was the Nautilus. She was twenty-one feet long, seven feet in diameter. Under water her propellor was driven by hand, on the surface she was propelled by a sail attached to a collapsible mast. She was submerged by flooding interior tanks. On her first trial at Brest the Nautilus proved herself blowing up an old schooner anchored in the harbour by diving under her and fixing a charge which, wisely, was carried outside the sub. Notwithstanding this notable success, the French Ministry of Marine made it plain they were putting their money into more conventional sea power. It might fairly be said that the real year the French lost the Battle of Trafalgar was 1801.

The French, however, were not alone in their misjudgment. The British Admiralty and the U.S. Navy Department showed no interest in Fulton's designs and he turned his mind to the steamship. In this field he was more successful. In 1815 he built the Fulton, the first steam-driven warship in the world, and no further attempts were made to design a submarine until the American Civil War.

The Confederate States built a number of small submersibles which were all called *David* – the *Goliath* presumably being the Yankee Navy which was blockading their ports. Driven by steam, they were not designed to dive fully but were trimmed down so that they went through the sea at 'deck level'.

Predictably it was not the most popular branch of the service. On 5 October, 1863, a *David* successfully attacked the Federal ship *New Ironsides* at Charleston. The *David* carried a single span torpedo strapped to her bows and she had to get so close to the ship for an accurate shot that she was swamped in the waves set up by the *Ironsides* as she sank.

An improved David was huyrriedly designed and put into service. The propellor, as with the first sub, was turned by hand by eight men in her crew while the ninth steered. Alas, she fared no better than her predecessor. On 7 February,

1864, she too was swamped when she sank the Federal ship *Housatonic* and went down with all hands.

Despite the overtones of opera bouffe, far-sighted Naval chiefs all over the world believed that underwater warships were the key to naval supremacy. They were prepared to pay a fortune to the inventor of the first successful submarine. The Russian government was to offer £144,000, the British £50,000.

An attack by a Russian torpedo boat on a Turkish Ironclad, which ended with the torpedo boat embedded in chain defences, first started Garrett's mind working on the submersible's problems.

It is savagely ironic that we owe that ultimate obscenity, the nuclear submarine, and the most vicious naval warfare which all but cost Britain her freedom and certainly the lives of countless of thousands of innocent civilians in two world wars to a Manchester clergyman's taste for riches.

When this irony was first pointed out in World War One, a number of clergymen, including his father, leapt to his defence. Their argument was that the deadlier the weapon of war, the better. For it would shorten war and save lives. It is an argument which, while it was become disastrously familiar in the years since then, would scarcely commend itself to, say, the citizens of Hiroshima.

The Revd Garrett, however, was concerned only with science and profit.

He first invented an air purifying apparatus which he fitted into an airtight case and demonstrated his faith in it by being shut in it under water for several hours. As a by-product, he invented a primitive diving suit which he called *Pneumatophore*.

Next the Reverend took out patents and, with J.T. Cochran, a shipbuilder of Duke Street, Birkinhead, he formed the Garrett Submarine Navigation and

Pneumatophore Company Limited to 'work certain inventions, consisting of a breathing apparatus, submarine torpedo boat, diving dress and Pneumatophore.' The company had a capital of £10,000.

The first submarine the company built at Birkinhead was only four and a half tons in weight. She was taken on secret trials in the Mersey.

A tugboat man who watched them remembered them some years later. He recalled: 'His favourite run was from the Grain Warehouse to the entrance of Egerton Dock. The submarine's movements were slow and you could tell where she was by the ripples she made on the surface. Now and then you would see her dome-shaped helmet come to the surface.'

A contemporary newspaper reported: ' . . . a torpedo boat invented by the Revd G.W. Garrett which has the power of sinking and remaining under water for many hours and thus can easily enter any blockaded port unperceived. The air is maintained at its normal composition by a chemical apparatus invented by Mr Garrett.'

The success of the prototype encouraged the Revd Garrett to greater things. His second submarine, the *Resurgam*, was powered by a steam boiler seven feet long and five feet high. Her pointed prow and stern were made of solid steel.

When she was launched, shortly after Garrett's twenty-seventh birthday, from the Alfred Dock, Birkenhead, on Wednesday, 10 December, 1879, it was only one year after Garrett had designed the first scale model and the Resurgam had taken only three weeks to build.

Her three-man crew consisted of Garrett, Captain Jackson, a master mariner, and George Price, an engineer.

Conditions for the crew were appalling. If the hull flooded it could only be pumped dry by hand. And to reach the pump the crewman would have to inch past the scorching boiler. On the surface the pilot had to stand on the boiler with his head stuck out of the conning tower. Inside her hull the temperature remained constant at 110 degrees fahrenheit.

The success of the prototype had generated interest in the Admiralty and the first trials in the Mersey so impressed naval observers – Garrett claimed he could submerge under power for five hours at a speed of three knots – that they offered to arrange official sea trials off Portsmouth in 1880.

A further inducement to carry on with the project came from Thorsten Nordenfeldt, the Norwegian inventor of the machine gun. Garrett was using a modified engine based on the Lamm design. Nordenfeldt was also planning to build submarines and he offered to take Garrett into partnership if the Portsmouth trials were a success. The profits on the machine gun would provide Garrett with much needed capital. He also needed the Norwegian's contacts with the war ministries of major European countries.

At 10.30 on a dark and foggy night the *Resurgam* was lowered into the water from the dockside and the adventure began.

The bad weather conditions made the cruise on the surface hazardous in the extreme and Captain Jackson was permanently on watch on the deck of the submarine as they cruised down river until they were clear of the other ships. Let Garrett take up the tale in his own words:

'We reached the Rock Lighthouse without accident of any sort and entered the Rock Channel. I took the helm in the conning tower but as soon as we were in the Channel Captain Jackson came inside, when we shut ourselves in and fairly started on our way.

We passed down the Rock Channel and, safely making Spencer's Spit, we turned into the Horse Channel which we cleared in due course and were then out to sea. We laid our course for the North West Lightship and went very slow, intending to make some experiments in Victoria Deep as soon as daylight should come.

When the morning of Thursday came there was very thick fog which prevented our making all the experiments we wished and necessitated our proceeding very carefully. The fog did not lift all day so we moved about, testing various parts of our interior machinery until Friday morning when the sun rose beautifully and clear.

We had now been at sea about 36 hours, a great deal of the time under water, and we felt desirous of making some port, as sleeping on board was not attended with such comfort as we wished.'

Engineer Price was to recall that they surfaced almost under the bows of a fully rigged sailing ship, homeward bound to Liverpool.

To the amazement of the skipper, Garrett lifted the conning tower hatch, hailed him and told him they had spent the last three hours under his keel.

'Where are you bound?' the skipper asked.

'In passage from Liverpool to Portsmouth,' he was told.

The skipper stared for a moment at Garrett's head, then his glare raked the tiny *Resurgam* from stem to stern.

'How many crew?' he asked.

'Three,' replied Garrett.

And the skipper delivered history's first verdict on the submarine service.

'Well,' he said, 'you are three of the biggest fools I have ever met.'

Garrett's log continues:

'At this time we found the North West Lightship close at hand, bearing about North, so we determined to put into the River Foryd as there is good anchorage there and she will dry out on every tide which is convenient as we were going to make a series of experiments. The boat answered splendidly in the sea way. The seas pass easily over her and cause hardly any motion. Nor do they interfere in any important degree with her steering.'

Safely ashore at Rhyl, there was a dispute with Cochran, the shipbuilder. The trials had been successful and he argued that at this stage they should be cautious. He wanted the *Resurgam* winched ashore and taken by road to Portsmouth. At this stage he felt it would be unwise, with a fortune within their grasp, to run the risk of losing her at sea.

The Revd Garrett insisted she should go by sea. But he agreed that she should be given an escort and Price was sent back to Birkenhead to bring back Garrett's steam yacht, *Elphin*, which, it was decided, would take her in tow for the rest of the passage.

Engineer Price was critical of Garrett's impatience when he steamed into Rhyl.

Common sense dictated that *Elphin* should undertake the difficult, narrow passage out of Rhyl in daylight. But Garrett was clearly anxious to get to Portsmouth. He was young and impetuous and, for all he knew, other sumbarine inventors might be hard on his heels. But his impatience was to cost him a fortune.

At 10 p.m. on Tuesday, 24 February, 1880, the *Resurgam* was towed out of Rhyl Harbour to the cheers of the fishing community. All that night they hugged the coast and by the next day they were nearing the Great Orme and Llandudno. But the weather was worsening rapidly. The barometer plunged and by 8 p.m. they were being buffeted by a full west-north-west gale.

Engineer Price remembered: 'Whilst off the Great Orme's Head the captain of the *Elphin* signalled to the *Resurgam* that they were in difficulties and unable to feed their boilers. They sent a boat across and we all three went over to the yacht, taking the submarine in tow. Garrett and Jackson went below whilst I went to the engine room to repair the pumps. During that time the gale sprang up and prevented us from returning to the submarine.

We towed her until 10 o'clock the following morning when she broke her hawser and we consequently lost her . . . '

The weather was so bad that no search could be made. Indeed, it was only with difficulty the *Elphin* made the Dee estuary where she dropped anchor off Mostyn.

Later that night there was more drama. The *Elphin* parted her chains and her crew came on deck to find they were being swept out to sea. They fired Verey lights and a steamer, the *Iron King*, came to her rescue. Unfortunately, in doing so, she rammed the *Elphin* and her crew had barely time to get on board the rescue ship before the *Elphin* sank.

Undaunted, Garrett hired a special train as soon as he was put ashore and returned to Liverpool to recruit a salvage crew. Unhappily the sea was now so rough that no boats could leave the Mersey and the whole adventure ended in failure.

Nevertheless, Garett had given sufficient proof of his ability for Nordenfeldt to take him into partnership. Garrett's modified engine was used in two submarines, one for Turkey and the other for Russia. In gratitude the Turks made Garrett a Bey, but neither submarine was to prove itself. It was almost as though the maritime gods had cursed this new vessel which was to bring such disaster to the seas over which they ruled. The engine in the submarine that the Turks bought proved unsatisfactory and the Russian submarine was lost under tow, eventually breaking up on Jutland.

Garrett's adventures continued. In 1890 he emigrated to the United States where the English parson, turned Turkish Bey, became a soldier. He fought for the Americans in Cuba in the Spanish American War. But he died peacefully in his bed in New York on 26 February, 1902. He was still only 50.

In October 1995, the *Resurgam* was finally found. /Carl Butler wrote in the Daily Post:

'The world's first mechanical submarine, which sank as it was being towed along the North Wales coast, has been found after more than 100 years. A Chester diver, Keith Hurley, discovered one of the region's most sought after wrecks, the *Resurgam*, by accident.

Train driver and maritime adventurer Mr Hurley, of Hoole, was untangling the nets of a Conwy fishing boat off Rhyl when he made the find of his life.

The 45-ft. long, 38-ton Resurgam, invented by Victorian curate Revd George Garrett and built by Cochran in Birkenhead, has been filmed and looks in good condition.

But the director of the Royal Navy Submarine Museum in Gosport, Commander Jeff Tall, pleaded for calm and caution last night. "The historical importance of Resurgam is very high. We do not want anyone messing about with it. It is a terrific story, terrific find, and my congratulations go to everyone involved. But our concern now is for its security."

Commander Tall added: "This is the first major discovery in the Mersey maritime area. The next step is one we will carefully weigh up. But it is our responsibility and we are already talking about safeguarding her and possibly lifting her. A major rescue operation is very much on the cards although a timescale is impossible to predict at this stage."

It is understood there would be a 50-50 split among maritime experts on the decision to mount a rescue operation. Some would rather keep the 45-ft. long, 38-ton submarine on the sea bed to preserve it there.

Commander Tall added: "Any long-term, on-shore rescue mission would involve extensive treatment with sodium carbonate. That is the same process which is preserving the Mary Rose in Portsmouth, to replace deep-sea salts which would erode the fabric of the metal. Much of the argument rests on affordability. If we suspect anyone trying to take parts of it, we will slap an historic wreck order on them."

Despite previous false alarms, Mr Hurley says this time he is '101 per cent' certain and Commander Tall agrees the find is the *Resurgam* (its name means I shall rise again).

Mr Hurley stumbled on the wreck as he was helping Dennis Hunt, whose fishing vessel, Patricia Dee, had its nets snagged.

When I went out, the water was unusually clear. When I went down I did not even consider the *Resurgam*, it was not on my mind. I followed the cable towards the nets and there was a huge blanket of fish which suggests there is a wreck. It was just as though a curtain split open and there suddenly in front of me was the *Resurgam*, there was no mistaking it. It was just as it looked in the old photographs. She was in excellent condition. She had gone down and not been seen since February, 1880, and I'm the first to see it. It was such a privilege. I took my glove off and touched it.'

Since then there have been alarming reports of theft from the *Resurgam* by rogue divers. Funds have still not been raised to rescue her.

Thirteen years after Garrett's death, in 1915, in the same stretch of the Celtic Sea in which the *Resurgam* had undergone her tests, her descendants, the U-boats, were active laying mines off the Welsh coast. One blew the *Alfred H. Read* to pieces, killing nineteen Liverpool pilots and Captain W.C. Poole who had commanded the Welsh immigrant ships to Patagonia.

In the same year the submarine that laid the mine had the dubious distinction of losing the last sea battle to be watched by spectators on land on the Isle of Man.

When the first World War broke out the Royal Navy had commandeered the tramp steamer *Argo*. Some months later she emerged from Plymouth dockyard outwardly unchanged from the tramp steamer which had plied between Garston and Bordeaux. She was, however, a vastly different vessel, the HMS *Lothbury*. Her crew of forty-three now included a master gunner, her skipper Wilkinson, a tough lieutenant commander who had served his time in windjammers, and, hidden in her holds, were a four-inch gun and two twelve-pounders.

Much of the First World War at sea seems to have been fought to a scenario written by John Buchan. The spies were more melodramatic, the battles have a larger-than-life aura. And, above all, nothing was quite what it seemed.

For the two fishing smacks that Wilkinson saw from his bridge, apparently trailing for mackerel in the narrow channel between Point of Ayre on the Isle of Man and Burrow Head on the Scottish isle of Whitham, were, in fact, two U-boats.

Dirty brown sails disguised their conning towers as they lay on the surface waiting for unarmed shipping. And if Wilkinson was mistaken, so were the skippers of the U-boats. For they took HMS *Lothbury* for easy prey.

Wilkinson's suspicions were aroused when he returned to the bridge after a ten-minute spell below to find that one fishing boat had vanished and the other was bearing down on him at a rate of knots that no fishing smack could make.

At 600 yards, the 'fishing smack' U-boat opened fire, spraying the *Lothbury*'s bridge with shrapnel. In doing so, she carelessly presented a perfect target to the 'coaster' gunboat. Bringing both the four-inch and his twelve-pounders into play, Wilkinson's first salvo from his four-inch hit the submarine in the engine room, sinking her with all hands.

Wilkinson was steaming through the wreckage when the second submarine surfaced. As she broke the waves, her crew were running down the decks, still awash, to mount the forrard gun. Once again, a hail of shrapnel peppered the bridge, supplemented this time with gas shells.

Wilkinson, after his first victory, was anxious to bring down another bird with a second barrel. Bringing the *Lothbury* about, he bore down on the second U-boat, sending her sailors spinning, and a brisk battle followed. At length, after a two-hour fight in which Wilkinson fired over two hundred shells, the U-boat broke contact and fled with the *Lothbury* in pursuit. She was, of course, hopelessly outclassed and it was not long before she was dropping astern.

It occurred to Wilkinson that the U-boat might be leading them into a trap and he ordered a smokescreen to be laid. Unfortunately, in doing so, a rating managed to set the ship on fire and, with a column of flame shooting forty feet in the air, the Lothbury had to disengage, doubtless to the surprise of the U-boat skipper and the dismay of his audience on the Isle of Man, so as to put out the fire before it reached his magazine and the match ended with an 'own goal'.

The sea battle was a curious reprise of naval history. Crowds on the Isle of Man and the Scottish coast had watched 160 years earlier another naval battle in another war.

Francois Thurot was a native of Dunkirk who had served his apprenticeship on luggers trading out of Douglas, Isle of Man. When England and France went to war in 1756, the knowledge he had gather of British trade routes earned him the command of a privateer. He was so successful in this role that, by 1760, he had reached the rank of admiral. That same year, aboard the 44-gun *Marechal Bellisle*, with the 22-gun *Le Terpsichore* and the 32-gun *Le Blonde* in support, he had sailed into Belfast Lough and bombarded shore installations.

When this news reached the Royal Navy in Kinsale, RN Commander John Elliott put to sea in the 32-gun *Aeolos*, with two 36-gunners, the *Pallas* and the *Brilliant*, in support. The three ships chased the French out of the Lough and met in battle in the channel where the Lothbury was to take on the two U-boats a century and a half later.

The battle between Elliott's ships and Thurot's raiders did not end until the French admiral and 300 of his men had been killed. Only then did the French surrender, to be towed into Ramsey Bay by Manx fishermen.

No less a clergyman than Queen Victoria's chaplain had defended Parson Garrett's invention.

'They will make the war shorter,' he wrote to the Times, 'and so save lives.' In fact U-boats were responsible for two of the blackest deeds in the history of the Irish Sea, as the next chapter will show.

Sources: *Sea Breezes, the Journal of the CPR*
            Contemporary newspapers and periodicals

Chapter Six

'Devil Boats'

The first Irish Packet station was established in Holyhead in 1656 to carry mails from the British Court to the armies in Ireland. At first the mails were carried in Navy ships but, by the eighteenth century, sailing cutters like the Cork-built, 42-ton *Henrietta* had taken over from the Crown. In 1820 two paddle steamers, the *Ivanhoe* and the *Talbot*, ushered in the steam era, cutting the sailing time between Britain and Ireland to six hours.

In 1834 the Admiralty once again took over the mails, introducing another paddle steamer, the *Cuckoo*. Thirteen years later, during the sort of economy drive which was to become familiar to service chiefs in the next century, the service was returned to civilian hands. The mail service was divided between the City of Dublin steam Packet Company and the North Western Railway Company until the Steam Packet Company won the exclusive contract, leaving the Railway Company to concentrate on passenger traffic.

By this time the steam packet vessel, the SS *Prince Arthur*, was making the crossing in four and three-quarter hours and the fleet included four more ships, the *Ulster*, *Leinster*, *Munster* and *Connaught*.

The LNWR's passengers used the steamers *Anglia*, *Scotia* and *Hibernia*. But, thanks to patrolling U-boats, the fleets of both companies were cut in half in World War One.

For the LNWR it was merely the continuation of a run of appalling luck .

On 17 April, 1863, the company's paddle steamer, *Telegraph*, ran aground near South Stack. On 8 September, 1875, two of its ships, the *Edith* and the *Duchess of Sutherland*, collided at the end of Holyhead breakwater. A month later the LNWR paddle steamer, *Earl Spencer*, collided with a Llanelli steamer, the *Merlin*, which sank near the breakwater. On 31 October, 1883, the company's steamer, *Holyhead*, struck a German barque and both were sunk. On 4 January, 1887, the paddle steamer, *Banshee*, ran aground off Porth Tywyn and the steamer, *Eleanor*, which was sent to tow her off, was herself grounded on the same bank. A year later, almost to the day, the *Earl Spencer* was in trouble again when she went aground beyond Holyhead breakwater. In 1900 it was the *Eleanor*'s turn again. She rammed another of the company's vessels, the *Connemara*, which in turn, on 20 March, 1910, rammed and sank a cargo steamer off the Skerries. For the *Connemara* it was third time unlucky. On 3 November, 1916, she was rammed and sunk by a collier.

This run of bad luck continued when the Admiralty requistioned four ships from the jinxed line. By 1917 all had been sunk, two by mines and two by torpedoes.

The *Hibernia*, renamed the *Tara*, had set up a naval record, patrolling 60,000 miles in a year in the North Channel between Scotland and Ireland. But the *Tara*'s fame was to rest on a more spectacular exploit.

In 1916 she was sent to join the North Egyptian Coastal Patrol based on Alexandria. Inevitably she was torpedoed in the port of Sollum. The U-boat commander who sank her took the ninety-two survivors on board but he refused to land them under a flag of truce in a British port. Instead he handed them over to cut-throat Senoussi tribesmen.

The crew – some men were in their seventies – was then force-marched hundreds of miles across the Red Desert in Libya. They were rescued at last by the Duke of Westminster and the column of armoured Rolls Royces he had fitted out and commanded in the desert war.

When my book *Shipwrecks of Anglesey and the Lleyn* was

published, a reader, Maureen March, sent me a copy of a diary kept by her father who was second officer on the *Tara*. I found it very moving.

' . . . The torpedo struck the ship on the starboard side in the wake of the engine room, making a loud explosion, breaking the wireless aerial, smashing our boat, wrecking steerage stairs, blowing away portion of main deck, and throwing large quantities of wreckage high in the air. I was on the Bridge and in charge of the ship at the time of the *Tara*'s destruction. I knew beforehand that should a submarine be in the vicinity we were absolutely a simple target, simply because the given speed of the ship was only sixty revolutions per minute on the engines, making the ship go about seven or seven and a half miles an hour. I did the best that I could possibly do on hearing the lookout report, as well as seeing the torpedo coming at express speed. Telegraphs were rang Full Speed ahead instantly, but escape was impossible. Had the ship been going at a speed, say, of not less than twelve miles per hour, and precautions in the way of zigzagging taken, a different tale, no doubt, one could tell. It must have damaged the hull considerably, as the vessel sank in about five minutes. Shortly after the torpedo stuck, our Naval Captain ordered all boats away. The ship was then sinking rapidly, and the gunners were busily trying to hit the submarine's periscope. Captain Tanner, our Master, was on the Bridge immediately, and he rang the telegraphs to stop, but there was no reply from the engine room. Everyone there, no doubt, was instantly killed or drowned. Seeing the ship sinking rapidly, and a lot of confusion in No. 1 boat and no officer in it I sprang in, and ordered lowering immediately, expecting something to break at any second, owing to the big crowd in the boat. After reaching the water we had great difficulty in unhooking the forward tackle owing to the ship's way.

About two minutes or so after clearing the tackle the ship disappeared, going down stern first, taking with her eleven of our crew. Three boats cleared the port side, being the only boats that got away safely . . .

When the *Tara* sank, the boats containing the survivors were towed by U.35 to submarine base at Port Bardia, a small land- locked creek, well sheltered from all winds. Some of the survivors were carried on the submarine's deck, in order to make towage lighter, and we were treated kindly by her crew, being given biscuits, water, bandages, disinfectants, and some clothing - one member of *Tara*'s crew having on no clothing whatever when leaving the ship . . .

. . . At Port Bardia, Captain Tanner and myself had a few minutes' conversation with the Captain of the submarine. He spoke English fairly and once spent a holiday in the Isle of Wight. He blamed England for having caused the war, and asked 'Why did you begin it?' I suppose he was within his rights in making us prisoners of war under German flag as he did . . .

. . . He lowered the German flag down, unbent it, and then hoisted the Turkish flag, and then turning to the crowd on deck informed them that they were now prisoners of His Majesty the Sultan of Turkey. At Port Bardia he handed us over to Nury Pasha (brother of Enver Pasha, head of the Young Turk Party who was Commander-in-Chief of the Senoussi Army. At that time the Senoussi were nominally at peace with the British, so that it would seem we should not have been made prisoners of war, though we might have been regarded as interned prisoners in a neutral country . . .

. . . The Old Mullah (Black Priest) at Hakim Abiet Wells (a Nubian negro) was overbearing at times, worked the men too hard with insufficient food, and struck them with a rhinocerous hide whip if they rested. Occasionally he was unreasonable about wells which were in his charge, compelling us to use water from dirty wells for cooking and drinking, as well as for washing purposes, although camels were given water from clean wells. We usually boiled the water, and fortunately no evil results seemed to follow. Dysentery attacked us all with the exception of about five or six amongst the complement, irrespective of which well we used water from . . .

. . . We were slowly starving. The guards, no dubt, had the bulk of our food; we could hear them grinding barley day after day, and you may depend they were not likely to feel the pangs of hunger for some considerable time – goodness only knows how much of our rations they had stowed away, although they continuously told us that they were feeling hungry like ourselves . . . '

He kept notes on the period spent in Tripoli as a prisoner of war. The following are some of the entries:

'11th Day, Monday, 15 November. Breakfast boiled rice. 9 a.m. broke camp and marched till 4.15 p.m. carrying our own gear: ground very rough in places: camped in gully which was named the "Graving dock": goat killed for us: water supplied by Arabs. Four other prisoners joined us from S.S. *Moorina* which was sunk by gun fire by a German submarine (probably the same blighter that sank us) while on a voyage from Bombay to Marseilles with horses for Army. They were well clothed – of course they had ample time to clear ship. Mr Colsted, Chief Officer (one of the four) had some "Traveller" tobacco which he shared with us, and which was very acceptable. All of the *Tara*'s crew gave the four a rousing good cheer when they arrived. The goat we got came rather late, so we decided to keep it for the morrow. Slept on ledges overhung by rocks, which gave little shelter. Very draughty.

16th Day, Saturday, 20 November. Up early this morning. Boiled rice for breakfast. Thomas Owens, coal trimmer, missing – evidently strayed away during the night: not much hope of ever seeing him again. Ackmet Effendi very angry. Mustered all hands and counted us. Threatened to march us all day without food or water. Marched for ten hours with only a piece of biscuit and a drink of water. Everybody dead tired. Camped on open desert. Felling awfully hungry: feet blistered as usual.

21st Day, Thursday, 25 November. Flour and rice for breakfast. What a luxury! We made Arab bread or Flap Jacks, two each and enjoyed them. Noon, rice and water, and if you managed to keep one Arab bread, which was very tempting, of course you had it to your credit. 3.30 p.m. started again on the march and came to a halt at 9 p.m. Nothing to eat. Camped in open: bitterly cold; felt awfully tired.

22nd Day, Friday, 26 November. Called at 3 a.m. Very chilly. Boiled rice and water to eat for breakfast. Marched from 4 a.m. to 11 a.m. when we reached our destination – Wells of Hakim Abiet in the Libyan Desert. A cheerless looking place. What a blow and disappointment! We were stuffed up with the idea that this place was smothered with palm trees and date trees. The only things we could see were one well with water, one dry well, on small block house for Stores in which Ackmet Effendi will sleep. Wrote a letter home. Blowing hard all day. Had a little rice to eat. Camped in open desert, erecting small shelter walls to windward. There is a plentiful supply of water apparently, but the desert scrub does not look as if it will last long for firewood. Everyone fed up with the place.

33rd Day, Tuesday, 7 December. Breakfast boiled rice and a little green tea without sugar (or milk, of course). Rice is rather dirty and we have to pick it well before cooking. In afternoon more excitement as it was found that a young camel (about four months old) had fallen down well sometime during the night and was drowned. Captain Williams volunteered to go down and hook it on, thinking of course that he would get highly awarded for same. Hard lines. Capt. Ackmet, that sneak in charge of us, only gave him a hard biscuit. After hauling the camel up, Rowlands, Quartermaster, who used to be a butcher's boy, cut it up. Our mouths were watering during the operation, the meat looked so lovely and tender. For tea we had boiled rice and camel's head. Later on in the evening we made soup out of the camel's liver, kidneys and heart. Everyone had a good burst out; went to bed feeling well fed, and content after a fashion, but we had been rather hungry or would not have eaten drowned camel. But all the same we were all praying for a few more camels to fall into the same place. Sorry to say, though, great precautions were taken when large caravans were passing through.

43rd Day, Friday, 17 December. Breakfast, rice. We are all wondering what bread is like, not talking of bacon and eggs (oh my!) Thomas Owen, coal trimmer, who deserted us a month ago, was returned to camp under escort. Mahomet Effendi smacked his face two or three times, and put him down the disused well. He got a biscuit and some water and later on in the day Captain Williams managed to get him free from any further imprisonment. He had been found straying on the desert two days after deserting us, and was taken to Sollum, and was apparently kindly treated, and in the matter of food seems to have fared better than us. His escort brought us four sacks of rice. He was very lucky in not being shot, but I expect his clothes were not worth having; they took a shirt and pair of drawers off him. Soup for dinner, and the usual for tea. So ended the day; bed next, and the pot to look forward to next morning. All one thinks about is food, and looking forward to seeing the pot going on the fire.

95th Day, Monday, 7 February. Weather colder, but not unbearable. We managed to get a sheep today – why? because it was drowned, and we are in such a way that we will eat anything. I'm eating snails galore, and enjoy them under the circumstances. Anxiously waiting for news, good news. Same food – regarding the rice, enough to make one cry.

134th Day, Friday, 17 March, St Patrick's Day . . . About 3 p.m. I was busily cutting the flesh from a sheep's leg preparing same for our final meal. I wanted to get the bones cracked, when all of a sudden someone at the tent entrance shouted, "Come out here, chaps. The Arabs are greatly excited rushing from tent to another, and clearing off in a westerly direction in great speed." Half of us never bothered about going out to look – too much of a fag or waste of energy, but wondered at the same time what the excitement was about. Then someone shouted "Here's a motor car coming". Oh my, then a rush out only to see more and more of them coming – the first ones armoured cars. The first car shied off a little taking precautions, and evidently trying to make out who we were. However, that didn't last long before you saw two men in khaki spring up waving in reply to us, and up they came with a dash only to know that they were British. Well, we felt overjoyed with gladness, lots of men shedding tears with joy.'

* * *

The run of bad luck which dogged the railway company lasted longer but it was to a vessel of the Dublin Steam Packet Company that the greatest disaster befell.

I have told the story of the torpedoing of the SS *Leinster* in full in the earlier book. What follows is a brief reprise of what happened on 10 October, 1918.

The *Leinster* was the flagship of the line. She was a 3,000-tonner, her 9,000 horse power engine had a top speed of 24 knots, she was twin-screwed and she was in passage between Kingstown and Holyhead twice daily. Each passage took her two hours, 45 minutes.

After warnings by neutral contacts that she was a U-boat target, the Line's directors tried in vain to get the Ministry of Shipping to provide a naval escort.

When she was torpedoed as she sailed out of Kingstown with six hundred and eighty seven passengers and a crew of seventy, she was defenceless. She was twelve miles out when the torpedo ripped open her bows and exploded in the ship's sorting office where twenty-two GPO men were working. Only two escaped.

A survivor, who was on the next deck, told of flames gushing from the sorting office.

'The ladder out of the office was smashed and I could hear men shouting in the darkness. Water was flooding in and only one man, dripping wet, managed to get out.'

The second survivor was blown clean out of the sorting office on a freak blast wave.

The skipper, Captain Birch, had been hideously wounded. With one eye hanging down his cheek, he had nevertheless tried to make a run for the Irish coast. He nearly succeeded. Lifeboats, full of civilian passengers, swung on their davits but it seemed they would not have to be lowered.

Then the U-boat fired a second, unnecessary torpedo into the crippled ship. It struck the *Leinster* in the engine midships.

A survivor said later: 'But for the second torpedo the water-tight compartments would have kept us afloat until help arrived. Boats were being got out on the davits, a couple had been floated and were picking up survivors who had been thrown in the sea.

The second torpedo struck the ship not far from our lifeboat. It was the most awful spectacle I have ever witnessed and it happened in clear view of the boats.'

The *Leinster* was listing to port and nearly down by the gunwales of the fore part: the stern was high in the air, the propellors clean out of the water when the second torpedo struck. There was a terrific explosion followed by the splintering of decks. Plating, spars, coal, cinders, boats and rafts were all blown into the air in a black cloud. In the water, boats and rafts were lifted by the blast and smashed into driftwood. Everything was scattered in a great black cloud of burning oil and debris. Her funnel, boilers and engine rooms were blown to pieces. One moment she was a damaged, but still seaworthy, Royal Mail steamer, the next she had ceased to exist. Nothing was left but odds and ends of wreckage. The *Leinster* literally crumbled into ashes.

Rescue ships arrived within an hour but for most of the *Leinster*'s passengers and crew it was too late and their bodies floated in the swell.

Despite massive injuries, Captain Birch had swum to one of the boats. A survivor remembered: 'We were crowded and there was no room on the boat for him. But he was obviously in very great pain and eventually we lifted him half out of the water, half in the boat. When we were picked up it was very difficult to get from the lifeboat to the destroyer. We had to jump at the precise moment the waves lifted us level with the decks and hope the sailors caught us. I fell twice before I made it. Before I was taken below I saw the Captain still hanging half in, half out of the water. I never saw him again and I assume he was washed away to his death.'

The German Navy has a long tradition of bravery in the face of unarmed merchant men, a quality which has not always been evident when its captains have come up with enemy ships of war.

The *Leinster* was the fifth cross channel packet to be lost in the war. But the greatest single tragedy at sea caused by a U-boat was that of the *Lusitania*.

The dubious honour of having been the U-boat commander who killed the most non-combatants with a single torpedo is held by Kapitan-Lieutenant Walter Schwieger. It was he who sank the *Lusitania* on 7 May, 1915, with the loss of one thousand one hundred and ninety-eight lives.

At an inquest in London, held three days after the *Lusitania* was sunk off Old Head of Kinsale, a judge, Lord Mersey, gave the opinion that 'the act was done not merely with the intention of sinking the ship but also with the intention of destroying the lives of the people on board.' Returning a verdict of wilful murder, he listed Schwieger's score: Adults: passengers (male) 421, (female) 270: crew (male) 397, (female) 16. Children 59, infants 35.

On 19 June the Kaiser conferred the Order Pour le Merite on Schwieger. He was not to enjoy his celebrity long. Two years later he was killed when his next submarine, the U-88, left Kiel on 7 September, 1917. Shortly after he had dived off Horn's Reef there was a terrific explosion and neither Schwieger nor his infamous U-boat were ever seen again.

There were more medals, in worse taste, struck after this disaster than at any other time. After the ship was sunk a German steelworks produced 100 medallions to commemorate the sinking. One side shows the liner's decks packed with guns and a warplane. On the other a skeleton Cunard agent sells tickets to innocent passengers. The opportunity this presented was quickly seen by British propagandists who pressed two hundred and fifty thousand more to whip up anti-German sentiment.

There were enough warnings of what was to come before the *Lusitania* sailed from New York on 1 May, 1915. The German Embassy in Washington had taken space in a number of US newspapers to warn: 'Vessels flying the flag of Britain are subject to destruction. Persons entering the war zone encompassing the British Isles do so at their own risk.'

One of the passengers, the multi-millionaire Alfred G. Vanderbilt, was advised by an unknown friend: 'Have it on good authority the *Lusitania* is to be torpedoed. You had better cancel passage immediately.'

A number of other passengers received anonymous telegrams. They contained one word – 'Morte'. Twenty years later a New Yorker, Saul Abramowitz, who survived, disclosed that before he sailed he had received a telegram: 'Do not take the Lusitania she will be sunk'.

There is also a curious story which appeared in a Welsh language magazine. An Anglesey tramp steamer was returning to its home port of Holyhead on the day the *Lusitania* was torpedoed. A U-boat surfaced and, as the rule of the sea ordered, the captain came to the conning tower and hailed the steamer. He ordered her crew to abandon ship. As he was required to, he gave them food, made sure they had charts and a compass.

Then he said a curious thing before sinking her: 'I would like to take you nearer your destination but I have not time. I have a rendezvous at 2 p.m. off Kinsale Head.'

The U-boat was the U-20. Presumably the rendezvous was with the *Lusitania*. I have heard it suggested from different sources that the *Lusitania*'s timetable was deliberately leaked to the Germans in order to bring the U.S. into the war.

Certainly many warnings were ignored and, on May Day 1915, the *Lusitania*, three times winner of the Blue Riband for the fastest transatlantic crossing, set sail on her two hundredth crossing of the Atlantic. When she entered the war zone five days later off the coast of Eire, the precautions taken were so slight that they were noticed by few of the passengers. Libeboats were swung out on the davits and their covers removed. Even when, on 6 May, the Admiralty radioed a warning of U-boat activity, the captain of the *Lusitania* – and probably one of the few men aboard who knew she was carrying a secret cargo of munitions – remained imperturbable. He posted extra look-outs but he himself behaved extraordinarily. Admiralty instructions were that merchant ships in a war zone should maintain maximum speed, keep clear of headlands, steam in mid-channel and steer a zig-zag course. Instead the captain slowed to 19 knots and hugged the coast near the Coningbeg lightship. And this in an area where U-boats had been reported. He made a perfect target for Schwieger's U-20 running on the surface off the Old Head of Kinsale, County Cork, at the end of a week-long patrol during which he had sunk a schooner and three steamers off the Irish coast. Now, obligingly, the *Lusitania*, thirteen miles away, altered course towards him. She was a target it would be impossible to miss.

At 1.20 p.m. he wrote in his log: 'Starboard ahead four funnels and two masts of a steamer with course at right angles to us. The ship is made out to be a large steamer.'

He submerged, and at 2.10 p.m. fired the single torpedo which sank the liner. It struck her forrard on the starboard side, detonated inside the hull and set off a second massive explosion which may have been the munitions.

It took no more than eighteen minutes for the 762-ft. ship to sink in 315 feet of water. Her bows filled and passengers returning from lunch were entombed for ever in lifts when the power failed.

The heavy starboard list prevented the launch of the port lifeboats. Hundreds of passengers were thrown into the water, few survived. One group paddled to safety on a grand piano, others drowned at once. Only seven hundred and sixty-one people were saved. All but four of the thirty-nine infants who had sailed died.

There were brave men. Vanderbilt would not come on deck until he was properly dressed. He was last seen clutching a purple jewel case looking 'dressed for Ascot'.

Charles Frohman, the impressario who had backed and encouraged J.M. Barrie to write Peter Pan, refused a place in one of the lifeboats.

'Why fear death?' he asked, paraphrasing Peter Pan. 'It's the greatest adventure in life.'

There were some incredible rescues. Mrs Margaret Gwyer, a bride of three weeks, and her clergyman husband escaped in a lifeboat. But as the liner turned over Mrs Gwyer was knocked out of the boat. Her companions had given her up for lost when she was scooped up by one of the liner's four funnels and sucked into it as the ship went under. At that moment the explosion in the engine room shot her out of the funnel. She went up in the air and landed in the water a considerable distance from the lifeboat. She was covered in black oil and dust, was badly bruised and most of her clothes were torn off. The 18-year-old seaman, Ledlie Morton, who rescued her was later awarded the King's Medal for helping to save nearly one hundred people.

Captain Turner, who escaped by clinging to a chair, admitted years later that he had been warned.

'I was distinctly worried. I was advised by the Admiralty that I was to keep a mid-channel course. We learned by wireless that there were six submarines waiting for us in mid-channel. That was the chief reason I closed in on the coast, and I also gave orders for all portholes to be closed. I thought that if the ship were sunk nearer shore the top deck might be above water after she had settled, allowing the passengers to escape, but apparently that was not to be.'

He was certain she was struck twice.

'What ship,' he asked, 'however big, could withstand such wounds? I saw a ship which was beached after she had been torpedoed. There was a hole in her side 32ft. by 18ft. although she had been hit only once.'

It was the merest chance, he insisted, that he was saved.

'At ten minutes to two on the afternoon of the sinking, I was taking a four-point bearing which would have fixed the ship's position with mathematical certainty in about twenty minutes. At 2 o'clock I was relieved, and I was writing my log in my cabin when the baggage master appeared. "The men are waiting for you down in the baggage room, sir," he said.

The baggage had to be brought up by lift and nothing could be touched unless in an officer's presence. I had on my new uniform, and the baggage room was a dirty place, so I decided to change into an older suit before I went down. I had hardly completed the change when the torpedo struck. Not a soul in the baggage room was saved.

The twenty minutes which followed the hit are fixed in my memory. They were electric. A moment of confusion! The quieting of the passengers! Sharp orders! Then the boat stations!'

But although the engines were stopped, the way of the huge vessel kept her rushing through the water and Captain Turner dared not order the boats to be lowered in such conditions. The *Lusitania* was travelling at 18 knots when she was struck.

Captain Turner continued: "At last I heard the order: 'Lower away the boats; women and children first!' I was on the port side, the high side, when my first boat, with sixty-five passengers, was lowered 90 feet to the sea. The second boat contained one passenger – a man paralysed by fear. He ignored my order to get out. I told a sailor to lift the man out. The sailor leaped into the boat with an axe. 'Hop it,' he commanded. The order was obeyed promptly.

The third boat scraped heavily against the ship's side as it went down. I am afraid it must have developed bad leaks, possibly sinking. It was impossible to get the fourth boat off.

Then came the end. An all-swallowing wave was rushing up the boat deck, devouring passengers, boats, every object in its path. I jumped into the sea. I swam ten, maybe twenty, strokes when I dropped literally into a huge hole of water. Down and down I went, into the darkest depths. I knew by my bursting lungs that my end could not be far away.

Then a mighty roar deafened me. The dragging ceased. I was being hurled upward with a force even greater than that which had pulled me down. I was flung waist high into the outer world. I caught a fleeting glimpse of a mound of frothy sea, and I knew that was the *Lusitania*'s grave.

I was plucked round the neck by somebody but I sank again. I made for the surface once more. This time I came up under an overturned boat. Almost exhausted, I worked my way under the gunwale and, virtually semiconscious, I found my head again above water.

A seaman sitting astride the keel of the boat yanked me out of the sea as if I had been a stranded fish.

Many hands were clutching despairingly at the frail support, turning it round and round like a revolving drum. I dropped off and started swimming again. I encountered wreckage of a collapsible boat which had been stove in. It would not support me. I felt I could fight no farther.

And then I bumped into some water-tight tanks and it was only a moment before I had jammed them under the thwarts of the collapsible boat, keeping it afloat.'

Robert Barnes, a saloon waiter, helped the women and children up the companionway, then made his way to the stern and jumped off.

'All you think of at the moment is self-preservation,' he said later. 'You dive into the water and take a chance.'

Asked if he jumped into the water fully clothed, he

replied: 'I took my tunic off and my waistcoat, and rolled up the legs of my pants. I was not in a panic.'

Mr Barnes was lucky. He managed to clamber on to an upturned collapsible boat.

One of the awful things is that you don't know which way you are drifting – to or from any land,' he said.

As it happened, he was drifting away, but a trawler picked him and his companion up and they were saved. The worst time of all, he later recalled, was when they were drifting in the sea towards dusk. 'How long, you wondered, would this go on for?' he said.

There were no cooler men aboard than the wireless operators. In a little room near the captain's bridge they worked steadily, indifferent to all but the job in hand.

'SOS, SOS *Lusitania*,' the operators gave out the message, and, with telephones strapped to ears, waited. Replies came, not from one quarter but from several.

'Come at once, big list.'

In the rest of the liner excitement mounted but in the wireless room work went on as if nothing out of the ordinary had occurred.

Chief Operator Leith and Second Operator David McCormick were calm. They resolved to do all that was humanly possible for the men, women and children who were on board. A passenger who looked in for news found himself moving out chairs and throwing them overboard. The wireless men felt the ship was doomed and concentrated on getting to the water as many floating articles as they could.

Afterwards Mr McCormick recalled: 'the scenes that followed were terrible. I just heard a thud and immediately the ship took a substantial list. It was only later I realised it was a torpedo.'

He continued: 'There was no panic. Nothing of the kind

happened. Everybody, almost without exception, behaved splendidly. I never saw nor heard of any men taking the place of women and children in the boats. In fact, pretty nearly all the members of the crew jumped into the water at the last moment after having done all that they possibly could for the others.

There was no attempt at the dramatic and Mr Leith and I did not even say goodbye to one another. Fortunately we met in safety later. The engineers were quite calm. One of two in passing our door shook hands and said "goodbye" and most of the fireroom crowd adopted the same method of leaving the ship. The vessel had taken so great a list that they were able with ease to walk down what normally would have been a perpendicular side and step into the water.

Of course, not every passenger was taking things calmly. I saw three men who seemed to be almost distraught. They cried out "My God" over and over again, and used similar expressions as they stood there undecided what they should do.

I saw a man, too, who clung excitedly to everybody he met in his terror. These are isolated instances, however, and in no way represented the situation which was free from panic.

After I got into the water and got free of the suction I managed to get hold of something. It was a collapsible boat supported by air-tight tanks which kept it afloat, notwithstanding the water it contained. There must have been about fourteen people in that boat in the same position as myself. To keep the boat afloat it was necessary for each to take part in balancing it but there was so much rocking that one after another we fell off. Then would come the task of climbing aboard again.'

A Manchester builder, Charles Crossley, was lunching with his wife when the torpedo struck. When he and others rushed up on deck from the luncheon table they saw that hundreds, including stokers, trimmers and others must have been blown to atoms, as well as many women and children who were in the forward cabins.

'In my own case and in that of my wife,' said Mr Crossley, 'we lost absolutely everything. All our belongings, including our money, went down with the boat. After many boats had been pushed off, and after some of these had been turned in the sea, my wife and myself found places in a boat which contained eighty-two people. More than half of these were women, one or two of whom were pulled into the boat from the sea in an absolutely stark naked condition. Other women in the boat quickly helped these poor souls in their terror and distress.

Just when our boat got into the water, the *Lusitania* came right over and we only just pulled off in time to be clear of the falling vessel. We saw one lady sucked into one of the funnels of the ship, from which afterwards in some wonderful way she was ejected again. One of the boats near us picked her up and rescued her.

The wireless apparatus fell in pieces about our ears as we pulled away from the ship but, fortunately, nobody was injured by it. We were lucky in having two men of the crew in our boat who were used to handling one and we rowed about for some three and a quarter hours before being picked up by a fishing smack. Though land was only eight miles distant from where the wreck took place, no landing could have been effected there. We were twenty-five miles from Queenstown harbour, which was an impossible distance for a boat with eighty-two passengers in it.'

Mr Handel Hawkins of Oldham was one of three members of the orchestra to be saved.

'I was clinging to a rope by the side of the boat when she began to roll over and I dived off,' he said. 'A short distance away I turned for a last look at the doomed ship. Hundreds of horror-stricken passengers were huddled together on the slanting decks. Women and children were crying for help that could not be given. There were no rescue ships about at the time and those on deck were going to almost certain death.

'As the vessel was keeling over women and children were falling into the sea. Others were clinging as long as possible to anything they could reach. The sight of so many helpless people going to their doom was sickening and I had to turn away before the boat went down altogether.'

Mr Hawkins went on: 'We had just finished playing for lunch and had gone aft to the bandmaster's room when there was a terrific thud,' he said. 'Someone looked at his watch and it was just 2.10.

We rushed on deck where some of the women and children were crying and screaming. But there was no panic. I do not think that the people realised that the ship was going down.

We did what we could to get the boats lowered and the women and children into them. Soon afterwards I went into the first-class portion of the boat where I was given a lifebelt. Going to the starboard side, I saw a boat being launched and, as there seemed few people about, I thought I would take my chance and got into the boat. The boat fell perpendicularly and men, women and children were thrown into the sea. Most of them must have been drowned as the *Lusitania* went down shortly afterwards. Along with three or four others, I clung to the ropes for a time. Then, freeing myself, I jumped off and swam away.'

After swimming for about ten minutes, Mr Hawkins came to a boat which had about eighty people in it and, being badly bruised from the wreckage and exhausted, he was taken aboard semi-conscious. He soon recovered, however, and gave a hand with the oars. Shortly afterwards they transferred the passengers to a ship that had come upon the scene and returned to rescue others.

Mr and Mrs William Campbell were at lunch in the saloon when the liner was torpedoed. There was no time to get lifebelts from their cabin but they got into one of the boats that was being lowered. The ropes gave way and the boat dropped a considerable distance into the water, throwing out all the occupants. It was then that Mrs Campbell lost her husband. For some time she was in the water and only learnt afterwards how she came to be saved. One of the stewards, in diving to avoid a funnel of the sinking ship, caught his hands in something which proved to be Mrs Campbell's hair. In this way she was pulled to the surface and then placed upon a raft of some kind. Later she was rescued by a boat which also contained the captain of the *Lusitania*. They were then transferred to a vessel named the *Bluebell*, probably a trawler. It was 11 o'clock at night before they were landed at Queenstown.

Two passengers on the *Lusitania*, Elizabeth Hampshire and Florence Whitehead, had been on a visit to Miss Hampshire's brother who was formerly a chemist in Milton, Massachusetts. They were lunching about 2 p.m. when they felt a shock that seemed to shatter the vessel, followed by smashing glass. Rushing out on deck they saw boats being lowered. There was no time to obtain lifebelts but they were assisted into a boat.

The *Lusitania* disappeared while they were rowing about picking up survivors. Four children were thrown into their boat, two of them twins, whose parents were later picked up by another boat and brought to shore. As one end of the liner dipped down into the water the other rose to a great height. Just before the final plunge Miss Whitehead saw one of the passengers calmly and deliberately dive from the elevated end into the waves.

Mr Harold Taylor and his wife Lucy were on their honeymoon trip on the *Lusitania*. They were married the day before the liner left New York.

'At the time the ship was struck,' said Mr Taylor, 'my wife and I were in our cabin. We had started packing up as we thought the lights would be off in the evening. When the torpedo hit I knew at once what it was. I was thrown against the side of the cabin. Immediately we ran upstairs. I had put my trousers, shirt and collar on. We went into the dining saloon and found the boat was then listing heavily. Suddenly I thought of the lifebelts and went back into the cabin for them. When I returned we went on deck and I put one of the belts round my wife as we were running along towards the boats. I saw my wife safely in No. 15 boat, I think it was, but could not get in myself.

It was by now almost impossible to stand up. The other boats were filled to overflowing. I raced for the last one being lowered but this seemed to be full of the crew so I just had to stay on deck. About two minutes later she went down. She had tilted so much that I was standing with my back against the face of the deck and my heels braced against the rail. As she went under I felt the suction dragging me and I went down making circles. Then the suction ceased and I began to go up. I kicked about with my feet and waved my arms. I was practically exhausted but I still kept rising. I did not care then whether I lived or not. However, I found my head above water amidst all the wreckage and the shouting people. Fortunately, for I cannot swim, I came up alongside an empty water-logged boat and managed to scramble in. Then I saw a man holding two ladies in the water. I succeeded in pulling the ladies into the boat and the man got in himself. We also picked up two stewards and another man.

The bows of the boat were staved in and she was making

water all the time. We found a small bucket in the boat and got another that was floating by and with these we had to keep baling out. We were two and a half hours like this without moving an inch and, though they were up to the knees in water, the ladies worked splendidly at baling to keep us afloat. Eventually we saw some destroyers and about half an hour later one of them picked us up and landed us at Queenstown at about twenty minutes past nine.

Five minutes after getting ashore I saw my wife coming out of the Cunard offices. She was in a distracted state for she had seen me go down with the ship and felt sure I was lost.'

There were other happy endings, some many years later.

In 1915 Margaret O'Connell wrote home that she was sailing in the *Lusitania*. After the news of the loss of the ship no more letters were received from her and her mother and family assumed that she was among the many drowned.

But, at the last moment, Mrs O'Connell had altered her plans and stayed in America. In June 1938, more than twenty years later, she wrote a letter to her sister who wrote back asking her to return home.

'I had no idea my folks thought I was drowned,' said Mrs O'Connell. 'I didn't write back because I thought they were annoyed with me at breaking my promise to come to England but last Christmas I decided to write again and here I am.'

Mrs Clara Howett's sister Hephzibah was informed that Clara was dead. But fifty years later Hephzibah was at Manchester airport to meet her sister, aged 83 and still going strong.

'I caught measles just before the *Lusitania* was due to sail,' exlained Clara, 'but all my luggage was sunk with the boat.'

Rumours of treasures on the *Lusitania* began to grow after Captain Turner gave an interview to a newspaper in which he said: 'Is there any truth in the stories about treasure and ammunition in the *Lusitania*? Not gold, of course, but . . . '

He added: 'There must be a lot of money and jewellery in the purser's safes. I am quite sure of that. As for ammunition, there was a certain amount of rifle cartridges and unloaded shell cases but that was all shown on the ship's manifest.'

'What about your own safe, captain?' he was asked.

'There's £15 that belongs to me, that is all,' he laughed, 'but there is an old sextant I value. It is in the left hand drawer of my desk.'

Asked what he thought of the feasibility of the project to explore the *Lusitania* through a diving tube, the captain said: 'I see no reason for failure and I hope they get me back that sextant.'

Not everyone believed the captain when he said there was no gold. In 1923 the *Daily Dispatch* reported under the headline 'Mystery Ship's Trip to Salve Lusitania's Gold?': 'There was an air of mystery and adventure about the departure from Dover yesterday of the powerful salvage steamer Semper Paratus, with clearance papers for the North Atlantic.

Although no official information of the vessel's destination can be obtained, it is believed that her mission is to attempt to salve the gold, worth several million, which went down in the *Lusitania*.

Count Landi, part owner of the ship, is on board, with other salvage experts, but when questioned before sailing he would only admit that they "might" attempt to recover the Lusitania's gold.

The Count is the inventor of a special diving dress to enable divers to reach greater depths than has been possible in the past, and the ship carried the very latest types of salvage equipment.'

But it was not until 1935 that the wreck was found by the SS *Orphir*.

Sources: Contemporary newspaper accounts

Chapter Seven

Search for Treasure

The SS *Orphir*, reconditioned at a cost of £50,000 by the Argonaut Corporation, Glasgow, which hoped to salvage thousands of pounds' worth of bullion and valuables from the *Lusitania*, set off on the first stage of her voyage in June, 1935.

On board were three survivors of the *Lusitania* disaster - Mr Bestic, third officer, by then chief officer of the *Orphir*; Mr Chisholm, second steward, by then chief steward of the *Orphir*, who, at the time of the disaster, was standing beside Vanderbilt, the American millionaire who was among the victims; and Mr Grant, the carpenter.

Her skipper, Captain Russell, admitted: 'Nobody knows the exact position of the *Lusitania*. There has been talk of millions of pounds' worth of gold in her strong room, but that is pure fantasy, like many other stories about the vessel.'

Seven days later the approximate spot where the giant Cunarder went down was marked by a buoy and a white flag.

Cement blocks were attached to the buoy by a 55-fathoms cable which anchored it against the Atlantic swell. The spot marked was seven and three-quarter miles south by west, half-west, of the Old Head of Kinsale. It was the nearest that Captain Russell and Chief Officer Bestic could come to the probable grave of the torpedoed ship.

From the buoy the *Orphir* combed the ocean methodically until its depth-recording apparatus located the wreck.

On board the salvage ship was the *Iron Man*, the Tritonia diving dress, that would take down a diver to 'depths at which no man has hitherto worked'.

'In the mud at 330 feet below the surface,' a contemporary account ran, 'Mr James Jarratt, who tested the suit in Loch Ness, will be set to work examining the wreck. It may be found, after making a preliminary survey, that further equipment will be needed to get into the liner's holds and strong rooms.

One of the first of the more accessible objects that will be sought is the purser's safe, which is believed to contain a large quantity of valuables that were the property of some of the wealthy passengers.'

It was on the *Iron Man* that the Argonaut Corporation pinned its faith. The all-metal suit was said to withstand the pressure of the sea, enabling the diver to breathe air at atmospheric pressure. Three oxygen cylinders were strapped to the back of the suit and the supply of oxygen was conducted to the inside of the metal suit by means of metal tubes.

The *Iron Man*'s wrist, elbow, shoulder, knee and hip joints were constructed to work with perfect freedom at all depths. The 'hands' were pincers, manipulated by hand grips from inside the arms.

When he did make his descent to the *Lusitania*, Mr Jarratt was connected by telephone with those above. There were four windows in his suit and attached to the front was an electric torch. In very deep water a 3,000 candle-power light could be lowered to the diver.

The dress was lowered into the sea by a wire cable and, in case the cable should foul an obstruction, there was a device inside the suit by means of which the diver could cast off the cable. He had only to detach a heavy lead weight from the suit and he would rise to the surface.

On 30 October it was announced that Jarratt had found the wreck with the help of the *Orphir*'s echo-sounder. In the *Iron Man* diving suit, he walked on the slime-covered side of the great wreck and made out a line of huge rivets. The experts declared that there was no other wreck in those waters with rivets of such dimensions.

It was the first time that a wreck lying in 300 feet of water had been reached by a man in a flexible diving dress.

The first really determined attempt to 'harvest' the *Lusitania* was not made for another twenty-nine years. Until then, diving techniques were not adequate to the challenge.

In 1966 a former United States navy diver, Mr John Light, arrived in Kinsale expecting to dive on the *Lusitania* within six months. So remote were the chances of salvage that Mr Light, aged 36, from Boston, Massachussets, was able to buy the wreck for £1,000.

His plan was for a two-year operation to bring metal worth nearly one million pounds from the ocean bed. Two teams of four divers were to spend periods of fourteen days isolated inside the artificial atmosphere of a diving bell and 17-ft. pressurised chamber on board the salvage ship *Kinvarra*.

But it was not until 1969 that he was ready to go. Problems of getting special equipment and components had delayed him. Before setting out, however, he declared: 'There is no gold aboard the Lusitania which lies in 315 feet of water. There is, however, in excess of 1,500 tons of non-ferrous metals, at present bringing more than £400 a ton on the metal market.'

Mr Light said the prime object of his company was to prove that new methods of diving were financially feasible on a commercial basis.

'If we succeed,' he said, 'and I am sure we shall, it will mean that any underwater wreck, down to a depth at present of 750 feet, can be salvaged profitably.

If the methods are proved on the *Lusitania* where we encounter currents, very bad winds and all problems normally met in salvage operations, they will work anywhere.'

The system was known as 'saturation diving'. Divers breathed in an artificial atmosphere in which nitrogen was replaced by harmless helium until their lung tissues became saturated.

In September 1969 Mr Light had still not dived. By that time every piece of equipment he had brought to Kinsale had been replaced. He told reporters he did not anticipate making the actual attempt on the *Lusitania* until 1970.

'Things are going well at the moment except for the occasional problem or two and at long last I feel that we are getting somewhere,' he said.

He spoke of long delays which, he said, the public might find difficult to understand. 'You cannot make one mistake, just one mistake and that is it,' he said.

Among other things, the inside of the diving bell had been replaced. 'About the only thing we didn't replace is the shell of the bell itself,' admitted Mr Light.

Whether Mr Light was successful or not does not show in the records. His security was legendary. But the last word, many feel, had already been said on the *Lusitania* in 1968. Certainly a long embarrassment was ended.

For the *Lusitania* memorial at Cobh, Country Cork, was not completed until 13 July, 1968 – forty years after it was started and fifty-three years after the tragedy. On that day Donal Murphy, a Dublin architect, supervised the erection of a bronze 'Angel of Peace' which surmounted the figures of two weeping fishermen erected in 1953.

The angel figure, weighing 17 cwt. and standing seven feet high, is inscribed in Gaelic 'Peace in the name of God'. The fishermen figures symbolise those who helped in rescue operations. The momument is also a memorial to world peace.

The fishermen figures were created by Jerome Connor, an Irish-American who changed the design six times before it was at last cast in bronze. He died in 1943 and it was not until some years later that Mr Murphy and Mr David Frame, A Dublin solicitor, found the figures in a Dublin foundry yard.

Sources: Contemporary journals and newspapers

Chapter Eight

Fire!

The most dreaded call of all at sea is the word that heads this chapter. And it has never, perhaps, rung upon less suspecting ears than it did on 28 August, 1848, in the waters off the Great Orme.

With little to hope for at home, the eyes of the labouring classes were all turned towards the New World. As the 1,300-ton *Ocean Monarch* steamed out of the Mersey bound for Boston and the promised land of America, the 300 emigrants aboard were each of them closing a door on their old life and looking eagerly into the future.

They had waved goodbye to stay-at-home families at the quayside in Liverpool and watched the Napoleonic fort that guarded the estuary fade into the horizon as they dropped down the river. The *Ocean Monarch* had been towed down by tugs. Just beyond the Bar Ship, she slipped her town and began the voyage under her own steam.

The morning had been uneventful but, at noon, just as the skipper was thinking with relish of his pre-lunch pink gin, a steward brought him some surprising information.

A passenger, he said, had lit a fire in the aft ventilation.

By the time the captain got aft, smoke was pouring from a state room through an open door into the main after cabin. Soon the whole of the after end of the ship was ablaze and terrified passengers were crowding forward. As some edged along the bowsprit, others, panicking, pushed them off into the sea where they drowned, only to be followed by more passengers pushed off in their turn.

The only ship in the vicinity was a private steam yacht, *Queen of the Ocean*, whose owner, a man called Littledale who was Commodore of the Royal Mersey Yacht Club, was returning from the Beaumaris Regatta. He spent two hours by the blazing ship taking aboard survivors. But the time came when he could take on no more.

Fortunately, a larger vessel, the *New World*, steamed by. Seeing terrified passengers huddled on the *Ocean Monarch* afraid to jump, an American seaman, Frederick Jerome, tied a rope round his waist and swam over from the *New World* to the stricken ship.

Grabbing a line from the *Monarch*, he raised himself, hand over hand, until he reached the blazing deck. A nightmare sight met his eyes. Mothers and children, too terrified to move, stiff with fright, huddled in pathetic groups ringed by flames.

The records do not say how many passengers Jerome saved by tying his rope round their waists and lowering them from the blazing deck into the sea. But he stayed at his work of mercy until the flames became too much for him and, with only minutes to spare before the *Monarch* sank, he, too, jumped into the sea.

In recognition of his bravery, he was made a Freeman of the City of New York and Queen Victoria sent him 'a gift'.

The greatest sea tragedy in North Welsh waters is, of course, that of the *Royal Charter* bringing emigrants back from the Australian gold fields. More than four hundred and fifty souls perished when, eleven years after the disaster of the *Ocean Monarch*, the *Royal Charter* went down off the coast of Anglesey in the worst gale of the nineteenth century.

Fifty years later there was a macabre sequel. A perfectly preserved teacup from the *Charter* was brought up off the Anglesey coast in the nets of the Hoylake trawler *Fleetwing*. A few hours later, as she was returning with her trophy in a thick fog, the *Fleetwing* was sunk in collision with the Mersey Docks Board tug, *Beta*, In the same fog, only hours later, the

Beta herself was sunk by the Booth liner, *Ambrose*.

Treasure seekers are a resourceful crew. Inspiration comes from the strangest sources. In the case of one diver it was a visit to the cinema. In the *Western Mail* Rhodri Hornung reported:

'When Jim Phillips sat in the cinema and watched the film Titanic he had a brainwave.

The way in which the ill-fated liner split in half and then sank beneath the waves had been exactly what had happened to another, lesser-known wreck off the Pembrokeshire coast, the *Nimrod*.

As Jim Phillips and his diving colleagues from the Adventurous Diving club in Swansea watched the safe in the film spill out into the water and come to rest between the two sections of the boat, he realised that that was what must have happened to the Nimrod's missing cabinet, for which divers had been searching for years.

Weeks later the team was back at the wreck and within fourteen minutes had discovered the missing cabinet with its cache of silverware and cutlery almost intact.

The find was the culmination of thirty years' diving and researching shipwrecks for the 50-year-old from Swansea.

Although Jim has been diving all over the world, it has been the wrecks around the coast of Pembrokeshire which have always drawn him back.

Its often-treacherous rocks are known to have claimed more than five thousand vessels, many of which still lie in their watery graves around its coast.

The wrecks attract hundreds of divers every year from all over Britain and for them Jim Phillips has now drawn up a special chart pinpointing to hundred and sixty of the country's best-known wrecks. As well as their locations, he also earmarks the date on which they were lost and the cargo they are believed to have been carrying. Together with the story of twenty of the most fascinating wrecks, the chart thus also outlines Pembrokeshire's maritime history in miniature.

"I've always been interested in wrecks ever since I was a boy and my dad took me diving to the *Nimrod*," he said. "Ever since then I've been hooked."

His early experience led him to take up diving professionally and he travelled all over the world. But marriage and a family led him to settle down in Swansea and stick to Britain's shoreline. "Diving is becoming increasingly popular and Pembrokeshire attracts divers from all over the country," said Jim. "It's one of the best places to see wrecks. There's a variety of shipwrecks and visibility is much better than a lot of areas because of the fresh water coming in from the Atlantic and the lack of pollution."

'The oldest known wrecks date back to the time of the Vikings, found at the Smalls, to the most recent wreck of the 20ft. *Nintendo*, which was lost by famous French yachtsman Bruno Joudran last summer near St David's Head.

But the *Nimrod* is one of the most famous of Pembrokeshire's wrecks. The paddle steamer was lost in 1860 at St David's Head in one of the worst hurricanes of the century. All forty-five crew and passengers lost their lives under the eyes of local people who lined the cliff tops, but were unable to help because of the ferocity of the weather.

Although divers have found many artefacts from it over the years, its silverware and glassware remained undiscovered until last summer. And while Jim Phillips reckons there must be many more treasure waiting to be discovered out there, the thrill of diving, he says, is in the experience.

"It's like flying, although a lot slower. When you're underwater you're like a bird. Visiting the wrecks is like stepping into the past. In some of them you can even go back into the rooms as they once were. If you find treasure, well that's just a bonus, but it's not why we do it.' "

At sea, disaster multiplies in direct ratio to the power of the engines. Today sea disasters reach an epic scale undreamt of by our forefathers. Two great tankers, sister ships, disappeared in the South Atlantic within two years of each other; two more were sunk in explosions. And today's sea disasters have implications beyond those which affect the people on board the ships. The world lives under constant threat of pollution on a massive scale from these huge leviathans of the sea.

One brisk January day in 1979 the French oil tanker, *Betelguese*, was discharging her cargo at Gulf Oil's Whiddy Island terminal off Bantry Bay. The spectacle was one which brought little joy to the spectators on land. The Isle of Whiddy was the perfect site for a terminal if you happened to be working for an oil company.

Bantry Bay, besides being one of the most beautiful stretches of coastline in the whole of Eire, is a natural harbour with all-weather shelter and deep water anchorage. From there, the crude oil from the Middle East could be trans-shipped to Gulf refineries in Holland, Spain and Wales in smaller tankers.

But concerned people who lived in the Bay dreaded what they believed was an inevitable oil spill. The reality was much worse than even their deepest fears. Aboard the tanker the gauge showed that the job was half done, the tanker's cargo was being speedily pumped out. But if the job was nearly over, it was also at its most critical stage. The unpurged holds were filled with volatile gas. At this stage the tanker was little more than a floating, unprimed bomb.

Ten years earlier in 1969 three supertankers of more than 200,000 tons had exploded within a month of each other. They were Shell's *Mactra*, which caught fire after an explosion in the Mozambique channel; the *Morpessa*, which sank off Senegal; and the Norwegian tanker, *King Haakon VI*, which exploded off Liberia.

After the *Mactra* disaster, the British government held an inquiry which went on for forty-seven days. It was established that all three ships had been cleaning their tanks when the explosions occurred.

Subsequent research into the nature of the atmosphere in the tanker's hold and how it was altered by different levels of oil, water or air, brought alarming results. It was discovered that the crude oil gave off a form of gas which, as tanks emptied, made clouds. At the same time, water drops containing charges of static electricity could form on the sides of the tanks. If these charges combined to form a spark, then the tanker 'bomb' was primed. The forty-three members of the crew of the *Betelgeuse* – she was named after the brightest star in the constellation of Orion – had special reason to be careful

On New Year's Eve the 215,000-ton Greek tanker, *Andros Patria*, exploded off the coast of Spain, killing thirty and spilling 30,000 tons of her 150,000-ton cargo. A week later her oil was still being washed up on the Spanish coastline of Lugo Province, 60 miles east of Corunna. The coast had some of the finest fishing grounds in Spain, famous for squid, crab and shellfish. Now they were ruined. The crew of the *Betelgeuse* had been following the story as attempts were made to tow the *Patria* out to sea to a fleet of tankers which was waiting 200 miles off the coast of Portugal to transfer her remaining oil.

Little did they realise that their own 'living bomb' was to blow the *Andros Patria* right off the front pages.

The explosion, when it came at 1 a.m. after the *Betelgeuse* had discharged half her load, could be hear sixty miles away in Cork city. The town of Bantry literally rocked, and horrified onlookers watched a pall of smoke rise 8,000 feet in the air before it settled to cover more than thirty miles of coastline with its acrid fumes.

Afterwards, eye – or rather ear – witnesses spoke of hearing a small explosion followed by a large one before the fire broke out.

Flames and bodies shot hundreds of feet in the air as the rescue services got quickly under way. There was little they could do for the tanker. The explosion had split her in two and forty-three of her crew, including a woman nurse, were killed instantly. Their bodies, when they were fished out of the water, were so thickly coated in oil that they added two stones to their weight.

A firefighter later described the scene: 'You just could not believe the sight,' he said. 'It was unbelievable. It was the nearest thing I have seen to the Hollywood disaster film *The Towering Inferno*.

The whole place was in flames and there was smoke everywhere with, now and then, odd small explosions. And there was fear. Even among those who were doing the rescuing.'

For the fire had spread beyond the tanker. As fireballs were volleyed six hundred feet into the air, the flames crept along the jetty, eating it up, and then along the pipeline through which the oil had been flowing.

Fire teams and rescue services from all over Eire were arriving by this time, and with great heroism they managed to stop the blaze reaching eighteen storage tanks which held an estimated million gallons of fuel.

Tug manager James Hendry, manager of the Bantry Bay Towing Company, was alerted by the explosion which he heard at his home two miles from the scene. Once aboard his tug, he spent the rest of the night searching for survivors.

'We were running up and down the Bay but we found no one,' he said.

The scale of the disaster was so great – it was the worst fire in Eire's history and seven people died on shore in addition to the forty-three on board – that, after it, offshore terminals were thoroughly re-examined.

Off Anglesey, Shell had recently built an offshore unloading terminal. Said an oil company spokesman:

'The Anglesey terminal is two miles out to sea; Bantry Bay is a 10-year-old terminal in enclosed waters with massive storage capacity nearby. The Amlwch terminal ties up tankers far out to sea and the oil is pumped two miles under the sea, then a further two miles to storage tanks, protected by the terrain of Rhosgoch. It's not possible to say that no explosion could occur on any ship anywhere but the layout of Amlwch is designed to prevent the development of a Bantry Bay type of catastrophe.'

Despite these reassuring words many islanders remained unconvinced.

They read with interest the complaints of Sir Bernard Braine, the Conservative MP for South East Essex. He had been compaigning for more than fifteen years to improve safety measures on Canvey Island, one of the largest concentrations of refineries and gas plants in the world.

He told the House of Commons:

'Vast quantities of liquified gas, oil and chemicals are stored away at any one time on Canvey Island very close to people's homes. The Government know the extent of the risks. The Health and Safety report published last summer outlined them, but unfortunately declined to take the obvious step of recommending the removal of the major hazard, the methane terminal.'

Many of the inhabitants of Britain's offshore islands, uneasy at the wooing of the oil companies, shared in varying measure his concern.

Sources: Contemporary newspaper and Maritime Journals
Shipwrecks of the North Wales Coast by
Ivor Wynne Jones

Chapter Nine

The Welsh Captain Hornblower

Though he was never shipwrecked, no one has created more wrecks than Gwynedd's greatest, though least known, seaman, Captain Timothy Edwards – or, to give him his nickname in George III's Navy, *Old Hammer and Nails*.

Though Edwards was born in Cambridge, he was the descendant of centuries of Llŷn squires and became one himself when his uncle made him heir to the Nanhoron Estate near Aberdaron.

At 14, in December 1745, at the height of the Jacobite menace, Tim joined the frigate *Chesterfield* as 'Captain's servant', the recognised route to a naval commission. His first engagement with the enemy, and the first prize in which he was to share, was on 18 November, 1746. It was described in the log of his captain, William Gordon, who tempted two French privateers into action by letting his sails shake as a decoy.

'One gave chase hoisting English colours. I fired a shot at her. She hoisted French colours; then we fired briskly both upper and lower deck guns and small arms for the space of about half an hour. We received several shot. One in particular cut the bolt rope of the main topgallant sail and crippled the yard. She wore right away from the wind and made all the sail she could from us. We made sail after her but she "sailing better" got away . . . '

Seven hours later the *Chesterfield* caught up with its prey . . .

'Fired several shot on which she brought to . . . '

That brisk little engagement made Captain Gordon a hero to his young servant and Edwards followed him to his next ship, *Assistance*. Gordon obviously returned the feeling because he appointed Edwards midshipman. He was posted first to a frigate, then to the sloop, *Sphinx*, at £1 10s. a month. He sailed in May for Nova Scotia to found a new settlement with 2,576 settlers, 100 cows and sheep and goats. The new settlement became the great city of Halifax.

After five years and five months he returned to England and served six months in merchant vessels to qualify for the 'six years' sea time' that was necessary for entry to naval examination list. He spent some time with his father, who was rector of Monmouth, until he was commissioned on 6 February, 1755, at the age of 24, as 6th Lieutenant on *Ramillies*, a 1,689-tonner being refitted as Admiral Byng's flagship for the Mediterranean fleet.

Fortunately he was subsequently posted to the *Terrible* on passage back to Nova Scotia, on which he was now considered an expert. Fortunately, because Byng was shot after a court martial for losing a battle.

The *Terrible* was ordered to prevent the French fleet from reinforcing the fortress of Louisburg. She was successful though half the ship's company – one hundred and twenty-nine men – caught smallpox, from which fifty-one men died.

Edwards escaped the contagion, was promoted lieutenant and transferred to the 28-gun sloop *Tartar*. Her skipper was to become known throughout the Navy as Captain John 'Lucky' Lockhart because of the fourteen prizes he took with only one hundred and eighty men to share the prize money. Edwards' share was £813, the equivalent of ten years' pay.

Amongst the *Tartar*'s adventures was the pursuit and capture of a privateer whilst Lockhart was carrying a fortune – £40,000 in cash, the wages of Plymouth dockyard.

One of the strangest battles was fought with the *Duc d'Aigillion*, a 500-ton privateer with twenty-four 10-pound guns and two six-pounders.

A letter has survived from a Portsmouth correspondent, who wrote:

'Thomas Doneau, commander, a gallant sailor . . . would have fought his ship whilst she could swim but was compelled by his crew who threatened to shoot him to strike to the *Tartar* after an engagement of one hour, twelve minutes, in which *Tartar* fired broadsides and had only four men killed and one wounded. The privateer had fifty killed . . .

This morning she came into harbour saluted with the cheers of several ships as she passed them. This is the sixth privateer and the best that has been taken in this war.'

Edwards must have played a brave part. Lockhart subsequently signalled the Admiralty requesting promotion for him. He was successful and Edwards was made commander of the 313-ton sloop, *Favourite*. She mounted fourteen guns and had a crew of one hundred and twenty-five. She was stationed at Gibraltar where Edwards had numerous sea fights with the French.

His most successful engagement brought him promotion to Post Captain. In his first year in command he fell in with two French sail, one of them the *Valeur*, a 24-gunner.

'The enemy expected *Favourite* to attack on the larboard (port) side and prepared accordingly; this being perceived by Captain Edwards he attacked them on the starboard side which threw them into such confusion they never recovered from it during the action.'

Recalling the battle, the naval historian John Beatson wrote:

'Too much praise cannot be given to Captain Timothy Edwards for his bravery on this occasion; and so sensible was Admiral Boscawen of his great merit that when *Valeur* was purchased by the Government and put into commission he bestowed the command of her on Edwards.'

Comparisons with the fictional naval heroes Hornblower and Aubrey, indeed with Nelson himself, are inevitable. dwards' career was a succession of hair-raising adventures. This is his own account of a spying mission he undertook along the French coast:

'Friday, 4 July . . . I went up aloft and had a good view of the Inner Road of Toulon, over a low bank of land opposite the two Outer Rocks, as I drew near Cape Sepet, incoming under Dutch colours. I saw a hulk and two or three men of war of the line, with their lower masts in, in that same road.

A little before four, the French at their Lookout House hoisted a blue flag eight times. I kept a pendant of that colour up and I heard a bell to the NW as I passed close to the shore. I perceived men very busy about their batteries between the two Capes.

A quarter before six, Cape Sepet North two miles, there was at the same time a Tartane in French colours going in rowing, so near the shore that I distinguished the colour of the men's clothes . . .

. . . a fishing boat boarded me which I detained for intelligence. Who said the French Fleet consisting of 4 sial of the line and two frigates had sailed on the 21st June . . . The Admiral sent the *Jersey, Dunkirk* and *Vestal* to chase . . . I paid the fishermen for their fish.'

Nothing fazed this battle-happy Welsh Squire. He was ordered to make sail along the Barbary coast and set up a meeting in his city with the Bey of Algiers.

' . . . the Bey saluted me with seven guns. At four, I had my first audience with him, attended by Mr Aspinall, His Majesty's Consul General, and he presented the usual presents, beef, mutton etc.

16 February. Ordered the convoy into the Mole to disembark the Algerines' gift of cannon. The men were supplied with fresh beef.

17 February . . . demanded of the Bey the redemption of two English slaves, one of which he set at liberty.'

He also found time for a little spying.

' . . . examined the environs of this city and find it very easy of access by landing men about three miles to the castles in a sandy bay, where there is a good opportunity to bring cannon before the place and deprive the inhabitants of water by seizing the sourse of the aqueduct in the march.'

There was a slight glitch when his whip was forced to put to sea in a gale leaving its captain stranded on shore and a French ship sailing into port.

Captain Edwards was unruffled.

'26 February. The sea growing less at noon I went to the Bey attended with our Consul to demand satisfaction of the crew of an Algerian cruiser, just arrived, that had plundered an English ship at sea of money and other effects. Then a bag of silver and other effects was restored and the people remanded.'

Subsequently Edwards enlarged his action in a report to the Admiralty. The Bey had seen very expensive gifts from Britain and was not going to risk losing them. He summoned the corsair captain.

'He had her crew severally searched; and after a severe reprimand to the soldiers that were the principals, he found and restored five hundred German crowns, two pieces of English silver, some wearing apparel of little worth and a few firearms.'

There was the matter of the other English slave still unsettled. So back to the Bey went Edwards and came away with the second freed slave.

In 1762 Edwards was given command as temporary captain on the 60-gun fourth-rater *Florentine*. A year later he was promoted full captain to command a new frigate, the *Emerald*. He was delighted but his joy was short-lived.

Within a year he came ashore from the frigate *Emerald* and came to live on the Llŷn in a rented farm, Cerrog Bach at Nefyn. He cannot have been too downcast. He had accumulated £10,000 in prize money and his Uncle Richard made him heir to Nanhoron.

Uncle Richard was clearly delighted when Edwards, at 37, married 27-year-old Catherine, the only child of his friend and fellow Master in Chancery. Catherine brought a further £2,000 in cash, equivalent to twenty years' captain's pay.

They were to have five children in eight years before he was called back to the colours when the American War of Independence broke out. Re-mustered in 1778, he commanded the frigate *Cornwall* where, in the first year, he ordered twenty-four floggings. At the same time he and his wife were exchanging charming poetry. She wrote to him:

'My guardian angels their soft wings display
And guide you safe through ev'ry dangerous way
In every state may you most happy be
And tho far distant, sometime think of me.'

To which he replied:

'In truth and tenderness secure
The pangs of absence I'll endure
Content to quit my bosom's queen
While honour cheers the parting scene
For every lonely hour shall be
Employed, my fair, to think on thee.'

And, presumably, put his notebook away and stepped out to watch another flogging.

Under the command of her poetic captain, the frigate sailed first to New York and then on to the Caribbean and Grenada, which the French had invaded with thirty ships of war.

Cornwall sailed with twenty-one other ships. She was the first to endure fire in the subsequent action and was so cut to pieces she had to quit the line to repair the damage. She did not quit the battle. Indeed, she was making sail to get back in the fight when the damaged main mast crashed into the sea. Even so, she continued to engage the enemy as her crew repaired the mast and its rigging. She limped into harbour at St Kitts.

Edwards joined Admiral Rodney's fleet. More battles followed but, sadly, it was disease which killed him. esperately sick and with the *Cornwall* virtually shot from under him, Edwards was discharged. He was returning home to Catherine when he died of malaria.

The captain's log of the *Acteon*, in which he was travelling, reads:

'Wednesday, 12 July, 1780. Departed this life Captain Timothy Edwards Esq., late captain of HMS *Cornwall*, and by his death his country has lost an honest, gallant officer.'

A servant cut off a lock of Edwards' hair to give to Catherine and he was buried at sea to the salute of twenty minute guns.

No doubt the Admiralty sent a message of condolence to Catherine but when it arrived at Nanhoron she was already on her way to meet the *Acteon* at Falmouth. She always met her husband when his ship docked. She took only enough money for lodgings, relying on her husband to buy both their coach fares for the return home.

His death at sea had disastrous consequences. She had no money and the church to which she applied refused her help to pay her fare home to Wales. She had terrible difficulty getting home where a local shepherd consoled her by reading her the bible – in Welsh. The couple were both Welsh-speaking. Edwards had taught her.

* * *

I am indebted for the facts above to my old friend, the late David Ellison. A remarkable man. A retired school teacher and colonial officer who took a job as a supermarket shelf filler in his seventies to finance his passion, naval history.

One day a fellow member of the Naval Historical Research Association, of which Ellison was archivist, bought at an auction in Fife a mourning locket in silver and carved ivory which bore the inscription 'Captain Timothy Edwards RN. Died 12th July 1780 aged 49'.

It took Ellison three years to trace Edwards to his home on the Nanhoron estate on the Llŷn, now the home of a descendant, David Harden and his wife Bettina.

Invited to visit, Ellison was delighted to see a large portrait of Edwards. David told him: 'I have often wondered about him.'

Bettina, meanwhile, had found an 18th century gardening encyclopaedia which had been a wedding gift to the Edwardses. She recalls: 'Every piece of paper that wasn't printed on was used to record seed mixtures for the lawns; the fruit trees that were ordered from London; when he first planted a hedge and when he cut it. He must have had tremendous vision because the park, garden and woodland he made is not very different from what is here today.'

Bettina also found the jottings book in which Edwards and his wife had written their poems to each other. A remarkable man. After his ordeal in the *Terrible* when half the ship's company went down with smallpox, he had his own family inoculated with mild doses of the disease. No one knows where he got the idea because it happened several years before Jenner evolved his inoculation technique.

Edwards got his nickname *Hammer and Nails* from the occasion he had the White Ensign of his ship hammered to the mast so it could not be shot away.

There is a memorial to Edwards in the local chapel at

Llangian. Nearby is the small congregational chapel Catherine had built as a tribute to a congregational minister who befriended her in Falmouth when the local vicar had refused to help her.

From the date of the first postcard he sent, I looked on admiringly at Ellison's diligent research. He started with the naval record at the PRO where he was lucky enough to find the Edwards' marriage settlement with details of Catherine's Bedfordshire estate. He went through Edwards' ships' logs and forty of his letters to the Admiralty.

At last it was finished and Gwynedd Archives agreed to publish it. When some difficulties arose I was able to help him sort them out. Alas, the next letter I had from him was to tell me he had inoperable cancer and he died before publication of the book, copies of which can be obtained from Gwynedd County Archives

* * *

In days of old when men were bolder Beaumaris was a nest of piracy with leading families of the town involved. In 1625 Thomas Cheadle, a sprig of the local gentry, received a grant of pardon for piracy 'being young and seduced by others'. In the same year Bishop Lewis Bayley warned the king that in August 'a ship had sounded the NE coast of Anglesey and at the same time Hugh Owen of Gwenynog returned for a short time very gallant and full of gold. The Roman Catholics have sold their all and gone after him. The same party are audacious and a stranger has lately surveyed the havens.'

He claimed measures taken against pirates were insufficient and a hundred men could overrun the island. Three years later John Griffith, Vice-Admiral of North Wales, complained that the bishop was intruding on the rights of the Admiralty but a year after that Griffith was asking for help to free the coasts of Anglesey from an English pirate, which had taken two barques freighted with goods worth £2,000 and sundry passengers of quality.

Six years earlier the deputy lieutenants gave a reason for the lawlessness at sea. They asked permission to move ordnance from Beaumaris Castle to more vulnerable points on the island afflicted with sickness and poverty and bad harvests. The populace 'lay subject to the spoil of shipping bound for Ireland.'

It was plain where local opinion lay. In the same year, the Mayor of Chester, who was also Admiral of the Dee, an office the mayor still holds, had complained that Liverpool and Caernarfonshire had refused to pay £40 as a contribution against pirates.

Anglesey was not alone in attracting pirates. At the same time the English pirate was operating off Anglesey, a French pirate took forty ships off Milford Haven.

But Anglesey had a special attraction for the sea thieves. Holyhead was the port of Mail Packet Boats and the town provided lodgings for notables from the Court in London as they waited for a fair passage to Ireland. So infested were the seas that, in 1630, Sir Thomas Button sailed from Waterford with the Irish Fleet to free the passage between Dublin, Holyhead and Chester 'which was infested with a pirate'.

He was not entirely successfully. In 1631 a Holyhead Post barque was boarded and robbed by a Turkish pirate. Particularly audacious was a raid in the same year by Arab slavers on Holyhead. They rounded up one hundred and fifty people and took them off to the white slave markets of North Africa.

During the Civil War barques were continually menaced. In 1649 the Irish took another Post barque and four years later a naval vessel spent ten days trying to free the Strait of pirates. Merchants on both sides of the Celtic Sea suffered. A merchant in Dublin complained that four of his ships were taken, two off Holyhead and two run ashore. He claimed the enemy took all the goods, money and clothes and sent the masters on shore to obtain £50 from the churchwarden, a Major Swift, or the boats would be fired and sunk. Poor Major Swift appears to have suffered from both sides. In 1652 he had complained that the Admiralty had seized his Post barque when it was cast ashore.

After a brief peace privateering broke out again from 1688 when William of Orange landed, ousting the Stuart king James. After the Battle of Cap La Hogue, when the British destroyed a large French fleet, the remnants of the French navy were leased out as privateers. In 1692 two of the French vessels, the *Swift* and the *St Martin*, sailing out of St Malo under false colours, captured the Post barque *Grace* off Dublin. She was stripped and her bare hull handed back for a ransom of £50. The same year the town of Holyhead itself was held to ransom by French privateers who threatened to burn it to the ground. The town was saved by a providential storm. In 1694 the cruiser *Scarborough* surrendered to two French privateers who mustered a total of sixty-six guns.

Pirate activity was strengthened by the French wars. A Captain Bates of Holyhead wrote a poem *Griffith and Jenneth* about privateers who raided a seaside farm near the town, took off the farmer and slaughtered four sheep and two goats for their larder.

The French did not have the profitable trade to themselves. In Beaumaris, the Society of Ancient Britons fitted out the *St David* as a 36-gun privateer. She was commanded by a Captain Reeves Jones, who sailed her out of Beaumaris in April and returned a few days later with a French privateer, which, according to a report, 'she had taken after a smart engagement of two hours and a half. The French had twenty-nine men killed, and the Welsh five.'

143

This spirited trade ended in 1800 when the Admiralty built a mail pier and harbour but there is still much work to be done in recovering this fascinating chapter in Anglesey's maritime history.

No doubt at the forefront of such work will be Dr Cecil Jones, a pioneer marine archaeologist whose extra mural courses in Menai Bridge as part of the University of Wales Bangor, brought enthusiastic recruits by the score to the new science.

To Dr Jones goes the credit of discovering Wales' oldest wreck. In 1976 he was laying a trail on the bed of the Menai for sports divers interested in marine biology. Off Pwllfanogl he spotted a pile of slates measuring 32 by 18-ft which had become home to a flourishing colony of marine life. Of more interest, he soon discovered, were the slates themselves. It was not, as he had supposed, waste dumped from the quay nearby, which, up to the 19th century, had exported writing slates for schools all over the British Empire. This was obviously all that remained of one of those ships, presumably sunk in a storm.

There was no record of the wreck. The only way to date it was by the slates themselves. Here Dr Jones had a piece of luck. He was able to identify three cuts of slate from Pwllfanogl, a 'single' quarried locally from either Llanberis or Nantlle and split with a gouge rather than a chisel. The quality of the workmanship and tool marks suggested they were cut in the 14th/15th century. Dr Jones and his team excavated a trench across the mound on the sea bed. They discovered the 40,000 slates were stacked, seven high, on a bed of twigs. It was probably that weight which took the slate ship straight to the bottom.

Below Harlech Castle in Cardigan Bay a treacherous reef is littered with wrecks. South of the reef in 1998, divers, who later founded the Cae Nest Group, discovered stone blocks of marble the size of double beds and, nearby, iron guns and a bronze bell and further evidence of an interesting wreck.

Clearly the ship, whose remains and cargo they found, had sailed in one of the fleets which brought marble from the quarries of Carrara to build stately homes and churches in Britain. Her position suggested she had hit a pile of boulders whilst trying to run ashore in a heavy storm. There were eighteen main battery and eight smaller cast iron guns and ten wrought iron guns. The bell was dated 1677 and its decoration suggested it was intended for a church. Other finds on subsequent dives included a purse, cutlery, the remains of pistols and a rapier.

Since there are traces of a thousand wrecks in Liverpool Bay alone, who knows what interesting artefacts remain to be discovered.

Much of the marine archeological interest in Gwynedd at the time of writing was centred on the wreck of a sixteenth century, 21-ft. workboat. The wreck, a swan's nest of timbers, was being reassembled at Eddison Mission Energy's Electric Mountain Exhibition Centre at Llanberis. The work was being done by Douglas McElvogue, 27, a research fellow at the University of Wales Bangor, and Peter Murphy, 61, a retired power station engineer. The two-year project was financed by Eddison Mission Energy at the urging of Capel Aris, the company's Control and Instrumentation manager.

The timbers were discovered by an unnamed worker in 1979 when Llyn Peris was drained during the construction of Dinorwig hydro-electric pumped storage power station. It was one of four wrecks found, two of them pre-historic log boats.

They were excavated by a local archaeological group under the direction of a retired teacher and nautical historian Owain Roberts, a world authority on the rigging of boats in classical Greece and Rome. For many years they were stored in his garage at Amlwch, Anglesey, because he could find no one interested in their display. A lecture on the wrecks which he gave inspired Capel Aris to persuade his company to finance the restoration and exhibit a wreck with one of the log boats.

McElvogue explained: 'The boat we are rebuilding is a locally built wreck which would have been used for agricultural and small scale industrial use in the mid-16th century. It was not at first visible when the lake was drained in 1979 but, when slate waste was dumped there, it was pushed up out of the mud – like squeezing a tube of tooth paste.'

Eighty per cent of the boat's timbers were recovered in good order, though subsequently sun-dried and in consequence brittle. It is hoped to exhibit the boats at the Llanberis Centre by September 2000.

McElvogue said: 'It is of historic importance and probably the oldest of its type.'

Murphy, who sails with Port Dinorwig club and builds his own sailing dinghies, said when the project started: 'It's an exciting prospect for me because of my interest in boats. My other interest, which is in history, makes this a natural gravitation.'

Besides the restored boat, the two have made a 4-ft. by 5-ft. scale model in oak.

The recovery was the result of an astonishing piece of luck. Millions of tons of slate waste were poured into the bed of the lake which lies under Dolbadarn Castle. The infilling stopped only two metres short of the wreck which would otherwise have been lost forever.

It is clinker built of Welsh oak, which is cleaved rather than sawn and fastened with hand forged iron nails. Animal droppings have been found amongst the timbers which suggest that animals were transported in it before it sank. It is believed the boat was used either to ferry farm animals along the lakes from the mountains to the winter lowland pastures or as a ferry operating between the lake ports at Cym y Glo and Nant Peris, taking travellers and their ponies to and from the bottom of the Llanberis Pass.

Sources: *Sea Raiders in the Waters Between Anglesey and Ireland during the 17 and 18th centuries* by Lucy Williams, Cymrodorion Transactions 1945.
Historic Shipwrecks by Valerie Fenwick and Alison Gale,1998.
Contemporary newspapers, the Dinorwic Project News and personal research for my BBC Wales progammes.

Chapter ten

Flotsam and Jetsam

A century ago little boys on Anglesey were warned 'You'll go to Clio'. It was enough to compel instant obedience.

Clio was an industrial training ship that was moored off Bangor from 1876 to 1919. She was one of a number of 'wooden wall' ships moored up and down the UK coastline. They took in boys who were beyond control, orphans and those from families too poor to feed and clothe them. Most of them left to join either the RN or the MN after their years on *Clio* which turned boys into men.

The *Clio* herself had an interesting history, which was put together piece by piece over three years by Emrys Roberts, deputy headmaster of Ysgol Gogarth, the North Wales School for Physically Handicapped Children. His interest sparked when he discovered that every year the boys from the *Clio* made their summer camp on the land on which his school was subsequently built.

She was commissioned for service on the Pacific Station in 1864. Aboard her, serving as midshipman, was Lord Charles Beresford, who wrote in his memoirs that the *Clio* was detailed to tow the store ship *Turtle* to Ascension in the South Atlantic. In passage, due to an error of judgement on the part of her first lieutenant, she ran down her charge, dismasted and nearly sank her. From Ascension, *Clio* shaped her course to the Falklands. Beresford wrote:

'The population consisted of Royal Marines, their wives and families, ranchers and South American gauchos. When *Clio* arrived, one of the gauchos was under sentence of death for the murder of one of the ranchers. The Governor arranged with *Clio*'s captain E.W. Turner for one of her crew to be hangsman.

When the bosun piped "Volunteers for a hangsman fall in" half the ship's company fell in. A Marine sergeant was chosen and taking a party ashore carried out the job.'

On her return voyage she brought Queen Emma, ruling Monarch of the Sandwich Isles, to visit Queen Victoria.

After forty-three years as a school the *Clio* was towed to Christiana Jetty where she was broken up for firewood. What is left of her keel can be seen off the Ja Ja jetty in Bangor at low tide.

The school of Ocean Studies is a department of the University of Wales, Bangor at Menai Bridge where the study of one wreck could affect the whole concept of pollutants on beaches. In 1991 the SS *Kimia*, carrying 1,500 tons of sunflower oil, sank off Angelsey.

When the oil hit the island's tourism beaches it used the sand as aggregate and set like concrete. It was an environmental disaster. But it could mean the end of beach pollution. A shipping firm planning to fuel its fleet with bio-diesel oil asked Dr Stephen Mudge at the School of Ocean Sciences whether that would behave in a similar way.

He told me: 'It has great potential. It is a renewable fuel. You can grow it – rape seed oil is the classic bio-diesel. It is carbon neutral so there is no excess carbon dioxide going into the atmosphere. There is a plant to produce it being built in South Wales and around ten in the rest of the UK.

When I looked at it I discovered another property. It was an exceptionally good solvent for oils and greases. When you get an oil spill most of its components dissolve but you are left with a thick, black treacly substance. I discovered bio-diesel will dissolve the black treacly mass and all you will have to do is lift it off the beach. It could have cleared the Pembroke beaches after the *Sea Empress* disaster in a very short time. In fact, the earlier you use it, the better. The longer you leave the oil, the thicker it becomes.

The anticipated market for any such device is any coastal port or marine authority. You get a spill, you load a beach buggy up with bio-diesel and it would be just like mowing a lawn.'

Dr Mudge put together project proposals for the EU. He envisages a buggy that scoops the beach up ahead of it, washes it with bio-diesel, then puts the clean sand back. In theory two or three people could clean a whole beach.

He says: 'The chemistry is well established. We have done it here and we know it works. It's the mechanics that are the problem. All we have to do is put the chemistry into a mechanical device. The knock-on benefits are huge to both the economy and the environment. Probably measured in millions of pounds.'

Will he share it with the university and a scientist in the States who worked with him?

'If there is any money I do not think any would flow in my direction. I don't mind. I am just doing my job. As a lecturer, I teach, do research and administration. Part of the research is to develop down this line. I have been particularly successful in finding something that has an application. It is probable that there will be some knock-on for the university if we develop our buggies for driving on the beaches because there will be some contribution from each one of those which is sold.'

He was content with the recognition he got for the work. A trophy that is a metal cross between a rainbow and a series of oil pipes, it is the Enterprise Oil Herriot Watt Univesity Award, one of the most prestigious awards in his branch of science.

Dr James Scourse is interested in the history of oceans and the absolutely critical part they play in the earth's atmosphere.

He says: 'Understanding the past is the key to understanding the future. You may not have as many archaeological artefacts as you do on land but you do have something better.

Most of the material is recovered by drilling ships which drill through the sea bed and recover a long core of sediment. By studying the sediment in sequence of age I can go back three or four million years. In parts of the deep ocean there are sediments that start at the present day and go back sixty million years. If you have an ice age the surface may be covered in sea ice.'

Dr Scourse's studies have other results.

'Folk memories of drowned cities, Lyonesse, the Mabinogi stories, Atlantis, have kernels of truth. The coastline has changed much more rapidly than it does at the present time. The Russians believe the lost city of Atlantis is situated in the little shelf south-west of the Scillies. They contacted me to ask if we were interested but there have been a number of surveys in that area and nothing has been found.

The Great Flood is another matter. Eighteen thousand years ago global sea level was one hundred and twenty metres lower than it is at the moment. Menai Bridge would have been covered by many hundreds of metres of ice. The melting ice caused the sea level to rise. It reached its present level 5,000 years ago. The Black Sea has a narrow neck. In the Mediterranean the sea level would have risen sharply producing catastrophic flooding in the Black Sea. There is documentary evidence to suggest the Black Sea may have been the prototype for Noah's Flood. There were some important civilisations in the area which had to get out pretty quick. The people had to move a kilometre a day in order to escape. It's possible Noah's Flood had some basis in those happenings. They had to protect their animals and in places construct boats and there is some evidence that the event

151

contributed to the birth of farming, the Neolithic revolution. They had to conserve seed and animals and plant and farm elsewhere. Rising sea levels have had a profound affect on human development.'

New discoveries are being made all the time.

'The fundamental pacemaker which drives the earth's climate on the thousand-year scale is the astronomical position of the earth. Twenty-five years ago we did not know that. We know by studying well dated core from the sea bed how to co-relate ice ages and warm ages exactly and compare them with the calculated astronomical position of the earth records. Not only can we test the past we can predict the future.'

And look in the past. The story of the wreck of the ark on the slopes of Mount Ararat may not be fanciful after all.

The happiest discovery was made on the Llŷn Peninsula at Porth Ty Mawr on the morning of the 6 April, 1901, when villagers of Llangwnadl awoke to find the shore strewn with bottles of whisky, barrels of stout, pots, mats and crockery. They came from the wreck of the *Stuart* which had come ashore during the night. Thirty years later the story was told by a newspaperman Eddie Kenrick and I am indebted to the loan of it and for all the deatails that follow to John Griffith, a retired teacher and horticultural adviser who lives in Llangwnadl and has long been fascinated by the story.

He loaned me photographs and showed me fragments of pottery from the wreck. His own parents could not share in the loot. They kept the Chapel House and, on the night of the wreck, the visiting minister, as was the custom, was staying with them before taking the service the next day in the chapel. But Mr Griffith did show me a photograph of a set of willow pattern cups and saucers, now in the possession of William Williams whose father worked on the land near Porth Colmon. Mr Williams lives at Twickenham and only uses them on the days that the Welsh team plays rugby there. Mr Griffith loaned me the faded newspaper cutting, which contains details not only of the wreck of the *Stuart* but of other goings on in that neighbourhood. It was by Eddie Kenrick, a colourful writer who deserves quoting at length.

'A century ago the smuggling of salt was rife along the Welsh coast. The price of salt was high above the price of many a poor man. On the Llŷn it was so prevalent that the Government appointed a deputy to watch over the coast. And when Mr Wilson came to take over his duties, times were lively.'

Mr Griffith recalls that three salt smugglers were caught and one escaped to hide in a milk churn at his mother's farm in Llangwnadl and eventually went to America.

Kenrick continues: 'The coast was patrolled from Nefyn to Aberdaron and smugglers grew more cautious and wary. Llŷn from its from its wild and remote position afforded a ready anchorage for smuggling craft. One of the best known smugglers in Llŷn was Red Hugh, a big hefty fellow, and he had quite a number of coves and shelters along the coast.'

Following in the wake of the smugglers came the searchers for wreckage on the sea shore. Ships lost their way and were drawn in and smashed upon the rocks. Then the villagers from miles around woke up. They rushed down to the shore in bodies and they garnered whatever they could.

'The old people will tell you some stirring tales about the *Stuart*. Whisky came ashore in cases. Pots, mats, furniture and foodstuffs. The whole neighbourhood flocked down and they got busy. Policemen who came on the scene were powerless to stop the scramble. Women carried away bottles of whisky in their blouses and, they say, with a finger to their lips, that a lot of the whisky is still buried in Llŷn. No one knows where. Perhaps those who buried it are long since dead. And the tale goes on to relate that half the neighbourhood was drunk for many days afterwards.'

The most precious of Mr Griffith's records was given to him by a neighbour, Hugh Jones. His mother was a daughter of Ty Mawr farm under whose cliffs the ship was wrecked and she took in a survivor, the Second Officer John Albert Camm, 26, from London. The captain, Logan Mitchison of Hull, was only 29 and blamed for his lack of experience. Mr Jones' account reads:

'April 6th 1901. The *Stuart* left Liverpool on Good Friday bound for Wellington and Dunedin, New Zealand. The tug left us some time during the night off Holyhead. The wind was head on. She went on a tack toward the Irish Coast and by noon on Saturday was coming around near Ireland. Then she steered a course towards the Welsh coast again with the intention of clearing Bardsey on this tack. However she was sailing faster than they thought. She was a clipper that had made a record passage from Australia. All the crew were new and young. Captain Mitchison, First Officer Alfred Samuel Blew, 25, Liverpool, and Second Officer T. Camm stayed at Brynbella, my home, for a fortnight after the wreck.

About 7 to 8 o'clock the Captain went below, leaving the first officer in charge with a look out for the Caernarfon lightship. About 9 o'clock the man on look out shouted: "Land ahead". The Captain was at once informed. He said, "It cannot be." However when he came on deck he found it was and gave orders to get the ship around but she misstayed and they had to wear ship.

'Afterwards they came along the coast. The weather was misty with drizzling rain. Before long she grounded on the rocks. Her keel crossed that of the *Sorrento* which was wrecked at the same spot in 1870. The crew of nineteen took to the lifeboats and were out all night. They drifted with the ebb tide and when daylight came they were out of sight of their ship. On rowing they came back to board her for dry clothes and food and came ashore with their belongings. It was thought that lack of experience was responsible for the disaster. At first it was thought that the ship could be refloated, but a few days pressure from the sea caused her mast to collapse and her cargo rendered available. It was soon scattered over the rocks. The fall of the mast having laid her open. Her cargo was mixed. Crockery, whisky, gowns, candles, matches etc. No lives were lost.'

The authorities did their best. Mr Griffith has preserved copies of despatches that were sent to the owners from salvage agents. They provide a dramatic picture.

The first message was from the Liverpool Salvage Association on 9 April at 2 p.m.

'*Stuart* lying quarter of a mile west of Porth Colmon on rock, heading north-east, broadside to sea and listing seaward 8 degrees. Depth of water alongside 10 feet out 7 amidships, 6 forward at low water. Nil feet more high water. Ground very uneven, large boulder through bottom between main mast and after hatch, decks there set up four feet, beams and hold stanchions broken for a length of 20 feet. Hull otherwise showing signs of damage, water rising and falling in hold with tide. Sure to break up first strong wind from westward. Meantime holding together. Send small steamer to save cargo. In low water might fill ships deck and load steamer high water. Can do nothing landward except at heavy expenses. Too much sea to do anything but trying to save the stores.'

Liverpool, 12 April, 11.57 a.m. Liverpool Salvage Association report.

'Re. *Stuart*. Our officer advises us that yesterday fifty packages eathernware and hardware, also six pianos, five of which were almost dry. Representative Stephen was compelled to leave for shelter owing to strong NNE wind and seas . . . The vessel *Stuart* broke in three places . . . '

16 April: 'The *Stuart* broke in three places this morning, the wreck listed seawards, cargo washing out, scattered along the coast, for the most part smashed upon the rocks, endeavouring to salve all possible.

The barque *Stuart*. Pwllheli bound from Liverpool to New Zealand with general cargo, wrecked four miles north of Bardsey, crew saved.'

A signal from the owners' agent, Caernarfon: 'Stuart in bad position, otherwise prospects of salvage good. Lighters alongside awaiting instructions. The Liverpool Salvage Association has despatched a special officer to the barque.'

The *Sorrento*, which Mr Jones mentioned, was a fascinating tale which Eddie Kenrick told superbly:

'An old tradition on Llŷn was that the Irish would one day invade the shores of Wales. This was the remnant of an old legend handed down from generation to generation. It had been told so many times that the country people really believed it and they went hourly and daily in fear of their lives.'

'The American ship *Sorrento* came ashore in 1870. That was the time of the Franco German war. When the sailors came ashore all wet and dripping after their rough immersion and knocked on the farmhouse door at Ty Mawr, the old people were thunderstruck.

"Cadi, they have come at last," shouted the old grandmother to her daughter. "Who have?" replied she. "Why, the Irish of course," answered the old woman.

The old man lit a rushlight, unhooked an old musket from the chimney and stumbled towards the door. When he drew the bar the sailors came tumbling in, knocking the old musket out of his hands. They began speaking in English, a langauge the old man had never heard before. He replied in Welsh. Neither understood the other.

Then the captain drew a box of matches from his pocket.

He took three matches from the box. He then laid the box on the table with the three matches upright. In the language of the times he was telling the Welshman that the wreck was a three-masted ship. The whole affair ended happily with the drinking of whisky from a bottle the captain had in his pocket.'

By this time the admirable Mr Kenrick had got the bit between his teeth. He went on:

'Porth Ty Mawr has always had a bad reputation for shipwrecks. At Porth Colmon, which is only a short distance away, a Spanish vessel came ashore in a great gale many years ago (see Chapter 2). The vessel went by the name of the *Villa* and the old people thought she was a smuggler.

One of the drowned sailors was taken to the old church to be buried. The sexton, for some unforeseen reason, had dug the grave too short. When the villagers and the surviving crew lowered the coffin it stuck half way. One brawny Spaniard took a jump and landed on the coffin, presumably with the intention of hastening the burial.

The parson at the time, Mr Owen, was a big strong man. He seized the sailor by the nape of the neck and lifted him bodily out of the grave. The funeral service then went on peacefully and the poor sailor received the last rights of the church without interruption.'

Inevitably Mr Kenrick, whose reporter's skills I admire, picked up another story from the locals about the tragic *Cyprian* (see Chapter 3).

'It was a stormy night and the cries of distress of the seamen could be heard far into the night. There is something tragic but fascinating in watching a vessel going to destruction. To see the torn sails, the ship being tossed this way and that, a helpless hulk.

So thought an old Welshman who had gone out to watch the ghastly scene. All through the night Welshmen kept watch with lanterns from the top of the cliffs. They were helpless to do anything. It was morning before the ship crashed on the rocks after a night as epic as any in the history of the sea. The sailors were nearly all drowned within sight of the shore. Only a few managed to come ashore.

The farmer was a pious old man and he proved a real 'trump'. He cared for the survivors and he helped to bury the dead. And then came calm days and the salving of the cargo. Silks, china, liquor, clothes. All things imaginable. People had been feverishly watching for days and now commenced the scramble. The stuff was safely carried home. Every house had to have its share and then the rumours spread that Customs Officers were coming to inspect each house to find a ship's cargo that had mysteriously disappeared.

The farmer was a generous man in a way but he had some miserly principles. He was not going to give up all he had won by dint of hard work. So whilst others placed their goods on hay stacks he thought of a better place to bury his treasure. He sought out a grave with a 'cist', opened the top and went back home for his goods. He buried the whole lot in the 'cist', then carefully replaced the stone. He went to bed chuckling because he thought he had thoroughly outwitted the Government officers.

Weeks and months went by. The threatened visit of the Customs Officers never materialised and then the old farmer, after some misgivings, thought it about time to unearth his treasure. He chose another dark night and he went to the churchyard. When he opened the "cist" he was amazed to find his silks had rotted to dust.'

I cannot resist lifting one final story from the admirable Eddie.

'There is one shipwreck that will always remain a mystery. It occured on the coast near Porth Ysgaden. The vessel seemed intact and when someone boarded it, they found a live pig in the hold and a watch ticking merrily away in the captain's cabin. Not a soul aboard her . . . '

Sources: John Griffith, Emrys Roberts (and, of course, Eddie Kenrick)